Trick of the Tale

THE

Trick

OF THE

Tale

Stories chosen by

Julia Eccleshare

VIKING

VIKING

Published by the Penguin Group
Penguin Books Ltd, 27 Wrights Lane, London W8 5TZ, England
Viking Penguin, a division of Penguin Books USA Inc.
375 Hudson Street, New York, New York 10014, USA
Penguin Books Australia Ltd, Ringwood, Victoria, Australia
Penguin Books Canada Ltd, 2801 John Street, Markham, Ontario, Canada L3R 1B4
Penguin Books (NZ) Ltd, 182–190 Wairau Road, Auckland 10, New Zealand

Penguin Books Ltd, Registered Offices: Harmondsworth, Middlesex, England

First published 1991
1 3 5 7 9 10 8 6 4 2

This collection copyright © Julia Eccleshare, 1991
The Acknowledgements on page 111 constitute an extension of this copyright page

Filmset in 11/14pt Baskerville

Printed in Great Britain by Butler & Tanner Ltd, Frome and London

A CIP catalogue record for this book is available from the British Library

ISBN 0–670–82454–2

Contents

A Christmas Pudding Improves with Keeping

PHILIPPA PEARCE

It was boiling-hot weather. The tall old house simmered and seethed in a late heat-wave. The Napper family shared the use of the garden, but today it was shadier and cooler for them to stay indoors, in their basement flat. There they lay about, breathless.

'I wish,' said Eddy, 'I wish – '

'Go on,' said his father. 'Wish for a private swimming-pool, or a private ice-cream fountain, or a private – ' He gave up, too hot.

'I wish – ' said Eddy, and stopped again.

'Go to the Park, Eddy,' said his mother. 'Ask if the dog upstairs would like a walk, and take him to the Park with you. See friends there. Try the swings for a bit of air.'

'No,' said Eddy. 'I wish I could make a Christmas pudding.'

His parents stared at him, too stupefied by heat to be properly amazed. He said: 'I know you always buy our Christmas pudding, Mum, but we could make one. It wouldn't be too early to make one now. We could. I wish we could.'

'Now?' said his mother faintly. 'In all this heat? And why? The bought puddings have always been all right, haven't they?'

'I remember,' said Mr Napper, 'my granny always made her own Christmas puddings. Always.'

'You and your granny!' said Mrs Napper.

'She made several at once. I remember them boiling away in her kitchen for hours and hours and hours. She made them early and stored them. When Christmas came, she served a pudding kept from the year before.' He sighed, smacked his lips. 'A Christmas pudding improves with keeping.'

Mrs Napper had closed her eyes, apparently in sleep; but Eddy was listening.

'We used to help with the puddings,' said Mr Napper. 'We all had a turn at stirring the mixture. You wished as you stirred, but you mustn't say what your wish was. And the wish came true before the next Christmas.'

'Yes,' cried Eddy. 'That's it! I want to stir and to wish – to wish – '

'Well,' said his mother with her eyes shut, 'if we ever make our own Christmas pudding, it won't be during a heat-wave.'

'I just wish – ' Eddy began again.

'Stop it, Eddy!' said his mother, waking up to be sharp. 'Go to the Park. Here's money for ice-cream.'

When Eddy had gone, his father said: 'That settled him!'

His mother said: 'The ideas they get! Come and gone in a minute, though . . .' They both dozed off.

But the idea that had come to Eddy did not go. Not at all.

The Nappers had moved into their basement flat in the spring of that year. Once, long before, the whole house had been one home for one well-off family, with servants, or a servant, in the basement kitchen. Later the house had been split up into flats, one floor to a flat, for separate families. Nowadays one family lived on the first floor, where the bedrooms had been. Another family lived on the ground floor, where the parlour and dining-room had been. (And this family owned a dog, and shared the garden with the Nappers.) And the Nappers themselves lived in the basement.

The conversion of the house into flats had been done many years before, but this was the first time since then – although the Nappers were not to know it – that a child had lived in the basement. Eddy was that child.

Ever since they'd moved into the basement, Eddy had had strange dreams. One dream, rather, and not a dream that his dreaming eyes saw, but something that he dreamt he heard. The sound was so slight, so indistinct, that at first even his dreaming self did not really notice it. *Swish – wish – wish!* it went. *Swish – wish – wish!* ... The dream-sound, even when he came to hear it properly, never woke him up in fright; indeed, it did not frighten him at all. To begin with, he did not even remember it when he woke up.

But – *Swish – wish – wish!* – the sound became more distinct as time passed, more insistent. Never loud, never threatening, however; but coaxing, cajoling, begging – begging and imploring –

'Please,' said Eddy to his mother, 'oh *please*! It's not a heat-wave now; it's nearly Christmas. And it's Saturday tomorrow: we've got all day. Can't we make our own Christmas pudding tomorrow? Please, please!'

'Oh, Eddy! I'm so busy!'

'You mean we can't?' Eddy looked as if he might cry. 'But we must! Oh, Mum, we must!'

'No, Eddy! And when I say no, I mean no!'

That evening, as they sat round the gas fire in their sitting-room, there was an alarming happening: a sudden rattle and clatter that seemed to start from above and come down and end in a crash – a crash not huge but evidently disastrous; and it was unmistakably in their own basement flat, in their own sitting-room.

9

And yet it wasn't.

Mrs Napper had sprung to her feet with a cry: 'Someone trying to break in!' Her eyes stared at the blank, wallpapered wall from which the crashing sound had seemed to come. There was nothing whatsoever to be seen; and now there was dead silence – except for the frantic barking of the dog upstairs. (The dog had been left on guard while his family went out, and he hadn't liked what he had just heard, any more than the Nappers had.)

Suddenly Eddy rushed to the wall and put his hands flat upon it. 'I wish – ' he cried. 'I wish – '

His father pulled him away. 'If there's anybody – or anything – there,' he said, 'I'll get at him.' He knocked furiously on the wall several times. Then he calmed himself and began rapping and tapping systematically, listening intently for any sound of hollowness, and swearing under his breath at the intrusive barking of the dog upstairs.

'Ah!' he said. 'At last!' He began scrabbling at the wallpaper with his pocket-knife and his fingernails. Layer upon layer of wallpaper began to be torn away.

'Whatever will the landlord say?' asked Mrs Napper, who had recovered her courage and some of her calm.

Mr Napper said: 'Eddy, get my tool-box. I don't know what may be under here.' While Eddy was gone, Mrs Napper fetched dust-sheets and spread them out against the mess.

What lay underneath all the ancient wallpapers was a small, squarish wooden door let into the wall at about waist-level: its knob was gone, but Mr Napper prized it open without too much difficulty. The dog upstairs was still barking; and, as soon as the little door was open, the sound came down to them with greater clearness.

With one hand Mr Napper was feeling through the doorway into the blackness inside. 'There's a shaft in here,' he said. 'It's not wide or deep from front to back, but it seems to go right up. I need the torch, Eddy.'

Even as Eddy came back with the torch, Mr Napper was saying cheerfully: 'We've been making a fuss about nothing. Why, this is just an old-fashioned service-lift, from the time our sitting-room was part of a big kitchen.'

'A lift?' Eddy repeated.

'Only a miniature one, for hauling food straight up from the kitchen to the dining-room and bringing the dirty dishes down again. It was worked by hand.'

Mrs Napper had not spoken. Now she said: 'What about all that rattling and the crash?'

Mr Napper was shining his torch into the shaft of the service-lift. 'The ropes for hauling up and down were rotten with age. They gave way at last. Yes, I can see the worn out ends of the cords.'

'But why should they choose to rot and break now?' asked Mrs Napper. 'Why *now?*'

'Why not now?' asked Mr Napper, closing that part of the discussion. He was still peering into the shaft. 'There was something on the service shelf when it fell. There are bits of broken china and – this – '

He brought out from the darkness of the square hole an odd-looking, dried-looking, black-looking object that sat on the palm of his hand like an irregularly shaped large ball.

'Ugh!' said Mrs Napper instantly.

Mr Napper said: 'It's just the remains of a ball of some-thing – a composite ball of something.' He picked at it with a finger-nail. 'Tiny bits all stuck and dried together . . .' He had worried out a fragment, and now he crumbled it in his hand. 'Look!'

Mrs Napper peered reluctantly over his shoulder. 'Well, I must say . . .'

11

'What is it?' asked Eddy; but suddenly he knew.

His mother had touched the crumblings, and then immediately wiped her fingers on a corner of dust-sheet. 'It looks like old, old sultanas and raisins and things ...'

'That's what I think,' said Mr Napper. 'It's a plum pudding. It *was* a plum pudding.'

Eddy had known: a Christmas pudding.

'But what was it doing there, in that service-lift thing?' asked Mrs Napper. 'Did someone leave it there deliberately or was it just mislaid? Was any of it eaten, do you think?'

'Hard to tell,' said Mr Napper.

'And why did the workmen leave it there when they sealed up the shaft to make the separate flats?' She was worrying at this mystery. 'Perhaps it was between floors and they didn't see it.'

'Or perhaps they didn't like to touch it,' said Eddy.

'Why do you say that?' his mother asked sharply.

'I don't know,' said Eddy.

They cleared up the mess as well as they could. The ancient pudding was wrapped in newspaper and put in the waste-bin under the kitchen sink.

Then it was time for Eddy to go to bed.

That night Eddy dreamt his dream more clearly than ever before. *Swish – wish – wish*! went whatever it was, round and round: *Swish – wish – wish*! In his dream he was dreaming the sound; and in his dream he opened his eyes and looked across a big old shadowy kitchen, past a towering dresser hung with jugs and stacked with plates and dishes on display, past a little wooden door to a service-lift, past a kitchen range with saucepans and a kettle on it –

His gaze reached the big kitchen table. Someone was standing at the table with his back to Eddy: a boy, just of Eddy's age and height, as far as he could tell. In fact, for an instant, Eddy had the strangest dream-sensation that he, Eddy, was standing there at the kitchen table. He, Eddy, was stirring a mixture of something dark and aromatic with a long wooden spoon in a big earthenware mixing-bowl – stirring round and round – stirring, stirring: *Swish – wish – wish ... Swish – wish – wish ...*

Wish! whispered the wooden spoon as it went round the bowl. *Wish! Wish!* But Eddy did not know what to wish. His not knowing made the boy at the table turn towards him; and when Eddy saw the boy's face, looked into his eyes, he knew. He knew everything, as though he were inside the boy, inside the boy's mind. He knew that this boy lived here in the basement; he was the child of the servant of the house. He helped his mother to cook the food that was put into the service-lift and hauled up to the dining-room upstairs. He helped her to serve the family who ate in the dining-room, and sat at their ease in the parlour, and slept in the comfortable bedrooms above. He hated the family that had to be served. He was filled with hatred as a bottle can be filled with poison.

The boy at the table was stirring a Christmas pudding for the family upstairs, and he was stirring into it his hatred and a wish –

Wish! whispered the wooden spoon. *Wish! Wish!* And the boy at the table smiled at Eddy, a secret and deadly little smile: they were two conspirators, or one boy. Either way, they were wishing, wishing ...

Someone screamed, and at that Eddy woke; and the screamer was Eddy himself. He tore out of his bed and his bedroom to where he could see a light in the little kitchen of the basement flat. There were his parents, in their dressing-gowns, drinking cups of tea. The kitchen clock said nearly three o'clock in the morning.

Eddy rushed into his mother's arms with a muddled, terrified account of a nightmare about a Christmas pudding. His mother soothed him, and looked over his head to his father. 'You said it was just coincidence that neither of us could sleep tonight for bad dreams. Is Eddy part of the coincidence, too?'

Mr Napper did not answer.

Mrs Napper said: 'That hateful, *hateful* old corpse of a pudding, or whatever it is, isn't going to spend another minute in my home.' She set Eddy aside so that she could go to the waste-bin under the sink.

'I'll take it outside,' said Mr Napper. 'I'll put it into the dustbin outside.' He was already easing his feet into his gardening shoes.

'The dustbin won't be cleared for another five days,' said Mrs Napper.

'Then I'll put it on the bonfire, and I'll burn it in the morning.'

'Without fail?'

'Without fail.'

Mr Napper carried the Christmas pudding, wrapped in old newspaper, out into the garden, and Eddy was sent back to bed by his mother. He lay awake in bed until he heard his father's footsteps coming back from the garden and into the flat. He didn't feel safe until he heard that.

Then he could go to sleep. But even then he slept lightly, anxiously. He heard the first of the cars in the road outside. Then he heard the people upstairs letting their dog out into the garden, as usual. The dog went bouncing and barking away into the distance, as it always did. Then he heard his parents getting up. And then – because he wanted to see the bonfire's first burning – to *witness it* – Eddy got up, too.

So Eddy was with his father when Mr Napper went to

light the bonfire. Indeed, Eddy was ahead of him on the narrow path, and he was carrying the box of matches.

'Whereabouts did you put the – the thing?' asked Eddy.

'The plum pudding? I put it on the very top of the bonfire.'

But it was not there. It had gone. There was a bit of crumpled old newspaper, but no pudding. Then Eddy saw why it had gone, and where. It had been dragged down from the top of the bonfire, and now it lay on the ground on the far side of the bonfire, partly eaten; and beside it lay the dog from the ground-floor flat. Eddy knew from the way the dog lay, and the absolute stillness of its body, that the dog was dead.

Mr Napper saw what Eddy saw.

Mr Napper said: 'Don't touch that dog, Eddy. Don't touch anything. I'm going back to tell them what's happened. You can come with me.'

But Eddy stayed by the bonfire because his feet seemed to have grown into the ground, and his father went back by himself. Alone, Eddy began to shiver; he wanted to cry; he wanted to scream. He knew what he wanted to do most of all. With trembling fingers he struck a match and lit the bonfire in several places. The heap was very dry and soon caught: it blazed merrily, forming glowing caves of fire within its heart. Eddy picked up the half-eaten Christmas pudding and flung it into one of the fiery caverns, and blue flames seemed to leap to welcome it and consume it.

Then Eddy began really to cry, and then felt his father's arms round him, holding him, comforting him, and heard the voice of his mother and then the lamentations of the family of the ground-floor flat, whose dog had been poisoned by what it had eaten.

And the bonfire flamed and blazed with flames like the flames of Hell.

The Fly

JOYCE DUNBAR

'Hey Dad! It nearly comes down to your chin!'

'Does that mean it's growing?' Harry's father lazily inquired.

'Of course it does!' said Harry. 'Can't you remember? It was only seven and a half centimetres when I first measured it – just past your nose. And now it's nearly nine!'

'Unbelievable,' said Harry's father. 'Now can I get on with my newspaper?'

'Hang on a minute,' said Harry. 'First a dose of Bay Rum. Then a bit of Mum's hair conditioner. Then mind you look after it.'

Harry's father good-naturedly submitted to the fussing and grooming. One thing was for sure: if it wasn't the longest devil's whisker in the world – it was certainly the most pampered.

'Mind you don't overdo it,' he cautioned.

Devil's whiskers ran in the family. Harry's grandfather had a few, curling up like horns from his thick bushy eyebrows, but none as long as this. Though Harry's father didn't admit it, he was rather proud of this extraordinarily long, bronze whisker bristling like a corkscrew from his brow. He told Harry that he was quite likely to have a devil's whisker of his own when he grew up.

But Harry couldn't wait that long. Not for nothing did he

lavish so much attention on a whisker. On it hung his own best hope – an entry in *The Guinness Book of Records*. The world's longest moustache was included – why not a devil's whisker?

Of course, Harry would much have preferred to set a record on his own account and had tried in all sorts of ways. He had spent nearly two hours patting his head and rubbing his belly at the same time – but had no reliable witness. He had taken three quarters of an hour to eat a single broad bean – but that was because he didn't like them so that didn't really count.

His mother said he must easily set the record for thinking of the daftest ways to set a record, but Harry didn't think that would do.

No. The best hope was the devil's whisker.

Or at least it was until the next day. Harry's father went to the barber's and a new girl cut his hair. 'You won't be wanting that will you sir?' she said, and with a quick flick of her wrist, snipped Harry's hopes in half.

Harry was furious! Though his father apologized profusely and said the whisker would grow again, Harry's face glowered like thunder.

'That whisker belonged to the devil!' he stormed.

'I shouldn't think the devil will care,' said his father.

'Oh yes he *might!*' rejoined Harry, before stomping off to his room.

'Red leather yellow leather,' he said, over and over again, trying to control his temper. 'Red leather yellow leather,' he chanted, all the way through lunch. '*Head reather yethow heller!*' he shouted, when his mother came to fetch him down.

She thought she'd better leave him to it. He was obviously trying to set a new record.

'Lead reather hello yeller,' he muttered, while his stomach hungrily rumbled.

It was then that he noticed the fly.

It was caught in a spider's web in the corner of his window. Despite its unusual size, its struggles only set the web shaking. Harry waited for the spider to emerge. He didn't think he would be able to watch. He knew that the scene would be gruesome.

Out it suddenly scuttled. Harry squinted through his half-closed fingers. In a split second the fly broke free and hopped on to the spider's back.

The spider seemed very perplexed. This way and that he scrambled, looking for the vanished fly. The fly just hung on tight. Then, through a series of extraordinary manoeuvres, the fly quickly trussed up the spider in its own web, waited for its struggles to subside, and calmly swallowed it down.

Harry blinked in amazement while the fly rubbed its forelegs together with the self-satisfied air of a mouse that has eaten a cat. What a turn of tables! A spider-eating fly! A diabolical fly!

The fly showed no intention of flying off so Harry reached for his magnifying glass and peered at the creature closely. He saw the great, plum-coloured eyes that took up most of the head. He saw the six, bristly legs and the oily, greeny-blue sheen of the body with its pair of transparent wings.

'Who's a pretty boy then?' said Harry with a shudder.

Then he noticed the devil's whiskers, sprouting between the fly's eyes. Magnificent devil's whiskers! This gave him an idea.

'If only I could catch him,' thought Harry, 'he might make it to *The Guinness Book of Records!*'

He belted off to the shed and found some empty jam jars gathering dust. One had a spider in the bottom. From the way it lay flat on its back with its legs arched stiffly in the air, Harry knew it was dead. Still, a fly wouldn't know. It was good enough for a fly to eat.

The fly was still where he left him. Using the dead spider as bait, Harry tried to coax the fly into the jar. 'Here you are. Big fat juicy spider. Come on. He's all yours.'

But this fly wasn't fooled. Although he crawled into the jar it took only the briefest investigation for him to realize that this spider was anything but juicy and to turn away in disdain.

Still, Harry had him caught. Now he had to keep him fed.

He had no luck at all catching spiders. He would have to try something else. 'What do flies eat?' he asked at tea-time.

'Anything,' said his mother in disgust. 'Absolutely anything and everything.'

Harry prepared a fly feast. Half a bruised banana. A bit of soggy bread. Ginger biscuit crumbs. He put it in the jar with the fly and pierced some holes in the lid. 'That should keep him happy for a while.'

It turned out to be a very short while. When Harry looked in the jar the next morning, there wasn't a bit of food left. The fly buzzed hungrily against the glass. He had grown at least four times in size!

Over the next few days Harry was very busy keeping his pet fly fed. Whatever he was given he ate, and whatever he ate made him bigger. When he'd reached the size of a mouse Harry transferred him to a shoe box, then to his old hamster cage. Still the fly kept on growing, making no attempt to escape. Although Harry found it difficult to read the expression in the bulbous, grid-like eyes, Harry thought the fly seemed happy.

19

But what a secret to keep! Harry found it more and more difficult.

'What's that noise?' said his mother one day when she was cleaning out his room.

'Me,' said Harry, 'I was humming.'

'That's funny,' said his mother, 'it sounded as if it came from the cupboard.'

Harry hummed for all he was worth.

'You're a bit quiet these days,' said his father one evening. 'I hope you're not still thinking of my whisker. I've told you it will grow again. Or you could try something else. If you really want to get into *The Guinness Book of Records* my lad, you should do it with something worthwhile.'

'Like what?' said Harry.

'Well – running the fastest mile. Jumping the highest jump. Keeping a kite in the air. Something that's a real achievement.'

'Well ... I *am* working on something at the moment,' said Harry. 'But it's a secret. Will you keep out of my room for a few days Mum? I want to give you a surprise.'

'Yes, if you make your own bed,' said his mother. Then, when Harry had closeted himself mysteriously away in his bedroom once again, she turned to her husband and said, 'Well that's a relief anyway. He's spent so much time in his room lately that I thought he was still in a sulk. I'm glad he's found a new interest.'

Harry's father just grunted suspiciously.

'Children need privacy just as much as adults,' said his mother.

One day Harry got a shock. His mother had been doing some baking when suddenly she turned round and said, 'Harry! Get rid of that fly!'

Harry froze, too startled to say a word. Then with one

of her floury hands she flicked a fly from the mixing-bowl.

'What's wrong with flies Mum?' asked Harry, after a heart-pounding pause. 'Why doesn't anyone like them?'

'Because they have filthy habits,' said his mother. 'They crawl all over everything. Over dung, over rubbish, over food. They spread germs!'

'But they must be here for a reason,' argued Harry.

'Well they're not,' said his mother emphatically. 'What was it somebody said?

> "The Lord in his wisdom made the fly
> And then forgot to tell us why."

– but I think the devil made flies!'

That evening, Harry took a bucket of soapy water, a brush and some 'Sparkle' into his room. By now the fly was as big as a small dog and lived in a battered old suitcase.

'I've got to clean you up,' he said to the fly. 'My mother says you have filthy habits.'

The fly resisted at first. Harry spoke soothingly to him. '*I* know you're different,' he said, gently starting to scrub, 'but I've got to convince other people.'

After that, the fly didn't mind. As Harry brushed and polished, he just couldn't help but marvel: at the enormous compound eyes gleaming like purple beacons, at the bristling devil's whiskers. Yes, he was rather grotesque – but at least he could be beautifully groomed! The fly soon got the idea, rubbing his body with his legs, cleaning his own antennae, blowing bubbles from the palps in his proboscis.

'How big are you going to get?' whispered Harry. 'When is it going to stop?'

When the fly was all spruced up Harry wondered if the moment had come: should he tell his mother and father?

But something made him uneasy. Although this was a prize fly, a fly like no other fly, something told him that his father might not be impressed, his mother might not be pleased.

'Besides,' he reasoned to the fly. 'You might not be fully grown. We want that record to beat all records.'

The fly seemed to nod in agreement, but from the way he bustled and buzzed, Harry thought he seemed troubled.

'What is it?' he asked. 'What are you trying to say?'

The fly's wings began to whirr. He paced the length of the bedroom, like an animal trapped in a cage.

'*Now* I understand,' exclaimed Harry. 'It's exercise! You want exercise! But it isn't going to be easy. Look, I won't put you back in the suitcase. Keep still under the bed, don't dare make a noise, and I'll take you for a walk this evening.'

At supper-time, more problems arose. 'Harry, have you been stealing from the larder?' asked his mother. 'The biscuits just seem to disappear and I'm sure there was some cake left in the tin.'

'No Mum,' mumbled Harry.

'There's even a cauliflower gone missing.'

'I don't like cauliflower,' said Harry truthfully.

'I know you're a growing boy and you can have as much food as you like – but just let me know what you're taking.'

'Yes Mum,' said Harry meekly.

'How's your project going?' asked his dad.

'Fine.'

'Not another daft idea?'

'No.'

'When are we going to hear about it?'

'Soon.'

That evening, when he was absolutely sure that his parents were absorbed in a television programme, Harry tied some cord round the fly's neck and led him down the stairs. The fly didn't make a sound. Harry led him into the street.

It was dusk, before the street lights were on. Other people were walking their dogs. Harry kept his distance from them but talked all the while to the fly.

'There, there. Steady boy. Steady. Not too fast.'

But the fly was pulling on the lead, pleased with his new-found freedom. His wings tried to stir into action, straining in their effort to beat.

Harry held on tight. The fly went faster and faster, skimming along the ground. At one point Harry stumbled. 'No. No. Stop! Down boy! Sit!' he hissed, trying to get to his feet.

He'd lost his devil's whisker. He couldn't bear to lose the fly as well, not after so much trouble. The fly was his winning entry and he *wasn't* letting it go!

Luckily for Harry, the fly found a packet of chips that someone had thrown away. Harry snatched them up and used them to lure the fly home.

'Phew,' he went, back in his bedroom. 'I won't do that again.'

Harry sat down on his bed while the fly finished off the chips. What a greedy guzzler he was! He got bigger before his eyes!

That night the fly was restless. He had grown too big for the suitcase and shuffled around the door.

'Shhhhhhh!' Harry kept saying, until he'd shushed himself off to sleep.

He woke up early next morning. His bedroom door stood open and the fly was nowhere to be seen.

Gosh! Oh horror of horrors! What if his parents should wake up to find a giant fly by the bed? Or if his mother should meet it on the landing?

Harry raced from his room. His parents' door was closed. Strange noises told him the way. Harry walked slowly downstairs until he came to the kitchen door. He hardly dared to look inside.

There was a rustling and rasping of paper, scuffling and scratching sounds. Harry opened the door just a crack.

The fly had been at it all night. He stood, filling the room, leg deep in empty packets. Tea, coffee, cornflakes, butter, sugar, spaghetti – the fly had eaten the lot. He was trying to start on the tins.

Harry heard footsteps above. His parents were getting up!

'What's the matter Harry?' said his mother.

Harry slammed the door and leaned against it.

'Don't Mum! Don't. Don't open the kitchen door!'

'Don't be silly Harry. Of course I'm going to open it. I've got to get the breakfast ready.'

'No! Mum! You mustn't go in there!'

'Out of the way Harry,' said his father. 'What are you playing at now?'

Harry saw that the game was up. He couldn't put it off any longer. He must make his amazing announcement.

'All right then,' he said. 'Are you ready? You might get a bit of a shock. Have you ever seen a thing like *this*?'

And then he flung open the door.

Somewhere, the devil was laughing. In his fingers was half a bronze whisker. Yes, it was his all right. And yes, oh yes, he cared.

Fabric Crafts

ANNE FINE

Alastair MacIntyre gripped his son Blair by the throat and shook him till his eyes bulged.

'Look here, laddie,' he hissed. 'I'm warning ye. One more time, say that one more time and whatever it is ye think ye're so good at, *whatever*, I'll have ye prove it!'

'You let go of Blair at once,' said Helen MacIntyre. 'His breakfast's getting cold on the table.'

Giving his son one last fierce shake, Alastair MacIntyre let go. Blair staggered backwards and caught his head against the spice shelf. Two or three little jars toppled over and the last of the turmeric puffed off the shelf and settled gently on his dark hair.

Alastair MacIntyre heard the crack of his son's head against the wood and looked up in anguish.

'Did ye hear that? Did ye hear that, Helen? He banged his head on yon shelf. He couldnae have done that a week back. The laddie's still growing! It'll be new trousers in another month. Och, I cannae bear it, Helen! I cannae bear to watch him sprouting out of a month's wages in clothes before my eyes. I'd raither watch breakfast telly!'

And picking up his plate, he left the room.

Blair fitted his long legs awkwardly under the table and rubbed his head.

'What was all that about?' he asked his mother. 'Why did he go berserk? What happened?'

'You said it again.'

'I didnae!'

'You did.'

'How? When?'

'You came downstairs, walked through the door, came up behind me at the stove, looked over my shoulder at the bacon in the pan, and you said it.'

'I didnae!'

'You did, lamb. You said: "I bet I could fit more slices of bacon into the pan than that." That's what you said. That's when he threw himself across the kitchen to throttle you.'

'I didnae hear myself.'

Helen MacIntyre put her hands on her son's shoulders and raised herself on to her tiptoes. She tried to blow the turmeric off his hair, but she wasn't tall enough.

'No. You don't hear yourself. And you don't think before you speak either. I reckon all your fine brains are draining away into your legs.'

'Blair doesnae have any brains.' Blair's younger sister, Annie, looked up from her crunchy granola. 'If he had any brains, he wouldnae say the things he does.'

'I dinnae say them,' Blair argued. 'They just come out. I dinnae even hear them when they're said!'

'There you are,' Annie crowed. 'That's what Mum said. All legs, no brain.'

She pushed her plate away across the table and dumped her school bag in its place. 'Tuesday. Have I got everything I need? Swimsuit, gymshorts, metalwork goggles, flute and embroidery.'

'Wheesht!' Blair warned. 'Keep your voice down.' But it was too late. The cheery litany had brought Alastair

MacIntyre back into the doorway like the dark avenging angel of some ancient, long-forgotten educational system.

'Are ye quite sure ye've no forgotten anything?' he asked his daughter with bitter sarcasm. 'Skis? Sunglasses? Archery set? Saddle and bridle, perhaps?'

'Och, no!' said Annie. 'I won't be needing any of them till it's our class's turn to go to Loch Tay.'

Alastair MacIntyre turned to his son.

'What about you, laddie? Are you all packed and ready for a long day in school? Climbing boots? Bee-keeping gear? Snorkel and oxygen tank?'

'Tuesday,' mused Blair. 'Only Fabric Crafts.'

'Fabric Crafts?'

'You know,' his wife explained to him. 'Sewing. That useful little skill you never learned.'

'Sewing? A laddie of mine sitting at his desk sewing?'

'Och, no, Dad. We dinnae sit at our desks. We have to share the silks and cottons. We sit round in a circle, and chat.'

'Sit in a circle and sew and chat?'

Blair backed away.

'Mam, he's turning rare red. I hope he's no' going to try again to strangle me!'

Alastair MacIntyre put his head in his hands.

'I cannae believe it,' he said in broken tones. 'My ain laddie, the son and grandson of miners, sits in a sewing circle and chats.'

'I dinnae just chat. I'm very good. I've started on embroidery now I've finished hemming my apron!'

Alastair MacIntyre groaned.

'His apron!'

'Dinnae take on so,' Helen MacIntyre comforted her husband. 'Everyone's son does it. The times are changing.'

She tipped a pile of greasy dishes into the sink and added: 'Thank God.'

'Not *my* son!' Alastair MacIntyre cried. 'Not *my* son! Not embroidery! No! I cannae bear it! I'm a reasonable man. I think I move with the times as fast as the next man. I didnae make a fuss when my ain lassie took up the metalwork. I didnae like it, but I bore with it. But there are limits. A man must have his sticking place, and this is mine. I willnae have my one and only son doing embroidery.'

'Why not?' demanded Blair. 'I'm very good at it. I bet I can embroider much, much better than wee Annie here.'

A terrible silence fell. Then Annie said:

'Ye said it again!'

Blair's eyes widened in horror.

'I didnae!'

'You did. We all heard ye. You said: "I bet I can embroider much, much better than wee Annie here!"'

'I didnae!'

'Ye did.'

'Mam?'

Mrs MacIntyre reached up and laid a comforting hand on his shoulder.

'Ye did, lamb. I'm sorry. I heard it, too.'

Suddenly Alastair MacIntyre looked as if an unpleasant thought had just struck him. He quickly recovered himself and began to whistle casually. He reached over to the draining board and picked up his lunch box. He slid his jacket off the peg behind the door, gave his wife a surreptitious little kiss on the cheek and started sidling towards the back door.

'Dad!'

Alastair MacIntyre pretended not to have heard.

'Hey, *Dad!*'

Even a deaf man would have felt the reverberations. Alastair MacIntyre admitted defeat. He turned back to his daughter.

'Yes, hen?'

'What about what you told him?'

'Who?'

'Blair.'

'What about, hen?'

'About what would happen if he said it again.'

Alastair MacIntyre looked like a hunted animal. He loosened his tie and cleared his throat, and still his voice came out all ragged.

'What did I say?'

'You said: "Say that one more time and whatever it is you think you're so good at, *whatever*, I'll have ye prove it." That's what you said.'

'Och, weel. This doesnae count. The laddie cannae prove he sews better than you.'

'Why not?'

'He just cannae.'

'He can, too. I'm entering my embroidery for the End-of-Term Competition. He can enter his.'

'Och, no, lassie!'

'Yes, Dad. You said so.'

'I was only joking.'

'Och, Dad! You were not!'

Alastair MacIntyre ran his finger around his collar to loosen it, and looked towards his wife for rescue.

'Helen?'

Annie folded her arms over her school bag and looked towards her mother for justice.

'Mam?'

Mrs MacIntyre turned away and slid her arms, as she'd

29

done every morning for the last nineteen years, into the greasy washing-up water.

'I think,' she said, 'it would be very good for him.'

Alastair MacIntyre stared in sheer disbelief at his wife's back. Then he slammed out. The heavy shudder of the door against the wooden frame dislodged loose plaster from the ceiling. Most of it fell on Blair, mingling quite nicely with the turmeric.

'Good for me, nothing,' said Blair. 'I'd enjoy it.'

'I didnae mean good for you,' admitted Mrs MacIntyre. 'I meant it would be good for your father.'

It was with the heaviest of hearts that Alastair MacIntyre returned from the pit head that evening to find his son perched on the doorstep, a small round embroidery frame in one hand, a needle in the other, mastering stem stitch.

'Have ye no' got anything better to do?' he asked his son irritably.

Blair turned his work over and bit off a loose end with practised ease.

'Och, Dad. Ye know I've only got a week. I'm going to have to work night and day as it is.'

Alastair MacIntyre took refuge in the kitchen. To try to cheer himself, he said to Helen:

'Wait till his friends drap in to find him ta'en up wi' yon rubbish. They'll take a rise out o' the laddie that will bring him back into his senses.'

'Jimmy and Iain were here already. He sent them along to The Work Box on Pitlochrie Street to buy another skein of Flaming Orange so he could finish off his border of french knots.'

The tea mug shook in Alastair MacIntyre's hand.

'Och, no,' he whispered.

Abandoning his tea, he strode back into the hall, only to find his son and his friends blocking the doorway as they held one skein of coloured embroidery floss after another up to the daylight.

'Ye cannae say that doesnae match. That's perfect, that is.'

'Ye maun be half blind! It's got a heap more red in it than the other.'

'It has not. It's as yellowy as the one he's run out of.'

'It is not.'

'What about that green, then? That's perfect, right?'

'Aye, that's unco' guid, that match.'

'Aye.'

Clutching his head, Alastair MacIntyre retreated.

The next day, Saturday, he felt better. Ensconced in his armchair in front of the rugby international on the television, his son at his side, he felt a happy man again – till he looked round.

Blair sat with his head down, stitching away with a rather fetching combination of Nectarine and Baby Blue.

'Will ye no' watch the match?' Alastair MacIntyre snapped at his son.

'I am watching,' said Blair. 'You should try watching telly and doing satin stitch. It's no' the easiest thing.'

Alastair MacIntyre tried to put it all out of his mind. France v. Scotland was not a match to spoil with parental disquiet. And when, in the last few moments, the beefy full back from Dunfermline converted the try that saved Scotland's bacon, he bounced in triumph on the springs of his chair and shouted in his joy:

'Och, did ye see that? Did ye see that!'

'Sorry,' said Blair. 'This coral stitch is the very de'il. Ye cannae simply stop and look up half-way through.'

31

All through the night, Alastair MacIntyre brooded. He brooded through his Sunday breakfast and brooded through his Sunday lunch. He brooded all through an afternoon's gardening and through most of supper. Then, over a second helping of prunes, he finally hatched out a plan.

The next evening, when he drove home from the pit head, instead of putting the car away in the garage he parked it in front of the house – a K-Registration Temptress – and went in search of his wayward son. He found him on the upstairs landing, fretting to Annie about whether his cross stitches were correctly aligned.

'Lay off that, laddie,' Alastair MacIntyre wheedled. 'Come out and help me tune up the car engine.'

Blair appeared not to have heard. He held his work up for his father's inspection.

'What do you reckon?' he said. 'Be honest. Dinnae spare my feelings. Do ye think those stitches in the China Blue are entirely regular? Now look very closely. I want ye to be picky.'

Alastair MacIntyre shuddered. Was this his son? He felt as if an incubus had taken hold of his first born.

'Blair,' he pleaded. 'Come out to the car. I need your help.'

'Take wee Annie,' Blair told him. 'She'll help ye. She got top marks in the car maintenance module. I cannae come.'

'Please, laddie.'

Alastair MacIntyre was almost in tears.

Blair rose. Extended to his full height, he towered over his father.

'Dad,' he said. 'Take wee Annie. I cannae come. I cannae risk getting oil ingrained in my fingers. It'll ruin my work.'

Barely stifling his sob of humiliation and outrage, Alastair

MacIntyre took the stairs three at a time on his way down and out to the nearest dark pub.

He came home to find wee Annie leaning over his engine, wiping her filthy hands on an oily rag.

'Ye've no' been looking after it at all well,' she scolded him. 'Your sparking plugs were a disgrace. And how long is it since you changed the oil, I'd like to know.'

Mortified, feeling a man among Martians, Alastair MacIntyre slunk through his own front door and up to his bed.

On the morning of the School Prize-Giving, Alastair MacIntyre woke feeling sick. He got no sympathy from his wife, who lay his suit out on the double bed.

Alastair MacIntyre put his head in his hands.

'I cannae bear it!' he said. 'I cannae bear it. My ain son, winning first prize for Fabric Crafts, for his sewing! I tell you, Helen. I cannae bear it!'

He was still muttering 'I cannae bear it' over and over to himself as the assistant head teacher ushered the two of them to their seats in the crowded school hall. The assistant head teacher patted him on the back in an encouraging fashion and told him: 'You maun be a very proud man today, Mr MacIntyre.'

Alastair MacIntyre sank on to his seat, close to tears.

He kept his eyes closed for most of the ceremony, opening them only when Annie was presented with the Junior Metalwork Prize, a new rasp. Here, to prove he was a man of the times as much as the next fellow, he clapped loudly and enthusiastically, then shut his eyes again directly, for fear of seeing his only son presented with a new pack of needles.

When the moment of truth came, he cracked and peeped.

Surreptitiously he peered around at the other parents.
Nobody was chortling. Nobody was whispering contemptuously to a neighbour. Nobody was so much as snickering quietly up a sleeve. So when everyone else clapped, he
clapped too, so as not to seem churlish.

Somebody leaned forward from the row behind and
tapped on his shoulder.

'I wadna say but what ye maun be a proud faither today,
Alastair MacIntyre.'

And raw as he was, he could discern no trace of sarcasm
in the remark.

As they filed out of the hall, Annie and Blair rejoined
them. Alastair MacIntyre congratulated his daughter. He
tried to follow up this success by congratulating his son, but
the words stuck in his throat. He was rescued by the arrival,
in shorts and shirts, of most of the school football team.

'Blair! Are ye no' ready yet? We're waitin' on ye!'

The goalie, a huge burly lad whose father worked at
the coal face at Alastair MacIntyre's pit, suddenly reached
forward and snatched at Blair's embroidery. Blair's father
shuddered. But all the goalie did was to fold it up neatly.

'A fair piece o' work, that,' he said. 'I saw it on display
in yon hall. I dinnae ken how ye managed all them fiddly
bits.'

'Och, it was nothing,' said Blair. 'I bet if you tried, you
could do one just as guid.'

Alastair MacIntyre stared at his son, then his wife, then
his daughter, then his son again.

'Och, no,' demurred the goalie. 'I couldnae manage that.
I've no' got your colour sense.'

He handed the embroidery to Alastair MacIntyre.

'Will ye keep hold o' that for him,' he said. 'He's got to
come and play football now. We cannae wait any longer.'

He turned to Annie. 'And you'll have to come too, wee Annie. Neil's awa' sick. You'll have to be the referee.'

Before she ran off, Annie dropped her new rasp into one of her father's pockets. Blair dropped a little packet into the other.

Alastair MacIntyre jumped as if scalded.

'What's in there?' he demanded, afraid to reach in and touch it in case it was a darning mushroom, or a new thimble.

'Iron-on letters,' Blair said. 'I asked for them. They're just the job for football shirts. We learned to iron in Home Economics. I'm going to fit up the whole football team.'

'What with?'

'KIRKCALDY KILLERS,' Blair told him proudly. 'In Flaming Orange and Baby Blue.'

Sonia Plays a Record

JON BLAKE

Many years ago we lived in a council flat, number 1B. Above us was another council flat, number 2B. The ceiling was very thin. A girl called Sonia lived in 2B, and every morning we heard her high heels going *clack clack clack* as she got ready for work. But that wasn't the worst thing. The worst thing was her pop records. Every time she put one on, Dad's fingernails would dig into the arms of his chair. Dad said that pop music was the lowest form of human expression. It destroyed your brain cells and turned you into a hooligan. We only listened to proper music. Classical music.

One day, we came home to find that Sonia had put on a new record.

'Oo,' said Mum. 'It's Elvis.'

'Who's Elvis?' snapped Dad.

'Come on now, Denis,' said Mum. 'Everyone's heard of Elvis Presley.'

'I am not *everyone*,' said Dad. 'I am an *individual*. And I am happy to say that I have never heard of Elvis Parsley, or whatever his name is.'

Dad disappeared behind his *Daily Telegraph* with a loud huff. I got out the chess set, and forced my little brother Nigel to play with me. Mum got out her knitting and sang absent-mindedly to herself:

'Caught in a trap,
I can't talk out,
Because I love you too much, ba–by!'

Dad lowered his *Daily Telegraph* and fixed her with his fiercest stare.

'What's the matter, love?' said Mum.

'You know what's the matter,' said Dad.

Mum shrugged and got back to her knitting. The record finished. Dad looked up towards heaven as if to give thanks. Then it started again. Dad began to fume. Nigel put his hands over his ears and rolled about like an idiot. I quickly changed the position of a few chess-pieces.

The record finished again. Dad gave thanks again. The record started again.

'There's something wrong with that girl,' said Dad.

'Perhaps she just likes the record,' said Mum.

'Impossible,' said Dad.

'Well, perhaps she's upset,' said Mum. 'Perhaps she's had an argument with her boyfriend.'

'What's that got to do with it?' asked Dad.

'Young girls often play records when they're upset,' said Mum.

'I've never heard anything so ridiculous in all my life,' said Dad.

Yet again the record stopped, and yet again it started. Nigel was beginning to pick up the words. Dad decided it was time for action.

'What's the number of the police station?' he demanded, picking up the phone.

'Oh, Denis!' said Mum. 'Surely you're not ringing the police?'

'Noise,' said Dad, 'is a criminal offence.'

'Can't you just go up and say something?' asked Mum.

'Such as?' said Dad.

'Ask her nicely to turn it down,' said Mum.

'Or play a *proper* record,' said Nigel.

'You keep out of this,' said Dad.

'What's the problem?' I said. 'You're not scared of telling her, are you, Dad?'

Dad's face froze. Slowly he put down the phone. He pulled up his shirt sleeves, strode across the room, and out into the hall. A few seconds later we heard our front door slam. Nigel and I jumped to our feet, scrambled after him, and put our ears to the door. Dad's great feet were clumping up the concrete steps towards 2B.

'She's for it now!' said Nigel, almost wetting himself with excitement.

'Ssh!' I said. 'I want to hear the screams.'

We waited a while, then a while longer. But we heard no screams, or breaking glass, or crashing furniture. All we heard was Elvis Parsley, singing just as loud as before. Nigel's giggles dried up, and a look of disappointment came over his face.

At last we could stand it no more. We opened the door, and crept up the stairs after Dad. We found him sitting on the upstairs landing, staring out of the window.

'I've been thinking,' he said. 'This is all your fault.'

Nigel's face dropped.

'Not just you, Nigel. Geoffrey as well.'

I smiled broadly, as I always do in these situations.

'She's fed up of listening to you two argue,' said Dad. 'Now she's getting her own back.'

Dad rose to his full height, and pointed his most menacing finger.

'*You* tell her to turn it off,' he ordered. 'And no tea till you've done it.'

Dad stamped off down the stairs and back into our flat. There was a moment's silence, while we imagined our fish fingers vanishing down the cat's gullet. Then I pushed Nigel towards the door.

'Go on then,' I said. 'Or are you chicken?'

Nigel answered my question by making a bolt for the stairs. I was ready for him. I tied him fast to the stair-rail with my belt, then knocked on Sonia's door and ran like hell.

Obviously the music was louder than I thought. Nobody answered the door. I tried knocking harder. Still no answer. For twenty minutes I knocked and ran, knocked and ran. Eventually Nigel struggled free. I decided to call it a day, and we went back downstairs to plead for our tea.

'And are you *sure* you knocked?' asked Dad.

'I *hammered* it, Dad,' I replied. 'Like a battering-ram.'

Dad gave Mum permission to give us our tea. But it was hard to swallow while Dad was pacing about the kitchen, like a caged lion.

'You know what's going on, don't you?' he said, eventually.

'What's that, Denis?' asked Mum.

'She's trying to drive us out, that's what,' said Dad.

'Why should she want to do that?' asked Mum.

'How should I know?' said Dad. 'She's probably got some pals on the council waiting-list. They're just waiting for us to move, then they'll be in here.'

'She always seemed such a nice girl,' said Mum, but Dad didn't seem to hear.

'If she wants war,' said Dad, 'war she shall have.'

Dad marched into the lounge. We abandoned our fish

39

fingers and followed. Dad went straight to the record cabinet.

'Let me see,' he said, sorting through the records. 'Borodin ... Brahms ... Beethoven ...'

'Beethoven's Fifth, Dad,' I suggested.

'Excellent choice, Geoffrey,' said Dad, and I felt a warm glow all over.

Dad put on the record, and turned the volume up. Mum shook her head. Nigel hid beneath a cushion. Suddenly Beethoven's masterpiece was blasting out of our tinny old stereo, and all my chess trophies were dancing up and down.

'Does it have to be quite so loud, Denis?' asked Mum.

'Yes!' raged Dad. 'Yes, it does!'

Dad strode to the window and struck a noble pose, while the great chords crashed around our ears.

'That'll show her, Dad!' I yelled.

'We-e-e-e-urgh!' gurgled Nigel, from beneath his cushion.

Twenty minutes later, the needle lifted. For a moment, there was total silence. It was eerie. We had forgotten what silence sounded like. Then, like some deadly curse, it was back:

> 'Caught in a trap,
> I can't walk out,
> Because I love you too much, ba–by!'

'Turn over the record, Geoffrey,' said Dad, keeping remarkably calm.

We were about half-way through the second side when Mum put her hand to her ear. 'I can hear something,' she said.

'It's called music, Mum,' I said, and Nigel laughed, and Mum got quite annoyed.

'I'm not talking about the music,' she said. 'I'm talking about the banging.'

We listened out. To our surprise, Mum was right. There was a steady *Thump! Thump! Thump!* coming from the wall.

'I think the people in 1C are knocking, Dad,' I said.

Dad ignored me. His eyes were closed and he was conducting with his little finger.

After a while the banging stopped. It was replaced by country-and-western music. It was very loud country-and-western music, louder than Elvis, even louder than Beethoven.

'They must have a jolly good hi-fi next door,' said Mum.

Dad's only response was to turn up the volume on our own stereo. But the volume was already on maximum, and the speakers were buzzing and fuzzing like they were about to explode.

'Are you going to go round next door, Dad?' asked Nigel.

Dad was still staring at our little stereo as if it had done him an injury.

'Couldn't we just go out for the evening?' pleaded Mum.

It was the worst thing Mum could have said. Dad was amazed.

'Give in?' he stormed. 'Give in, to these barbarians?'

'Never!' trilled Nigel.

'So they've got a big expensive show-off hi-fi,' said Dad. 'Well, we'll see if they've got *staying power* as well.'

Dad organized us all into shifts. Nigel was to keep the stereo going till eight, then I took over till eleven. Mum did the first night shift, and Dad took over at three a.m. to see us through until breakfast.

To be honest, I thought it would be all over before my shift started. But Sonia's record was still going strong at eleven p.m., and so was the country-and-western from 1C. I had to sleep with my head under my pillow and two wads of cotton-wool in my ears. I dreamt about Beethoven being caught in a trap on a cowboy ranch because he loved his baby too much.

Next morning all the records were blasting away as happily as before. I found Dad stretched out on the lounge carpet, with red eyes and a letter in his hand.

'Take this ... next door,' he mumbled, pushing the letter into my hand. 'I wrote it at five-thirty this morning.'

Dad was always telling me about the dying art of letter-writing. I decided I would stop off in the hall and read the letter, to see if I could learn anything.

The letter went like this:

YOU SCUM
Don't think I don't know what you're up to.
You're all in this together.
If you think you can get rid of us that easily, you've got another think coming.
You can stick your tasteless music where the monkey sticks its nuts.
Your neighbours,
The Farmer Family.

I was starting to seriously wonder if my dad really was the wisest man in the world. I crossed out 'The Farmer Family' and changed it to 'Denis Farmer'. Then I made the letter into a paper aeroplane so I could fire it through 1C's letter-box, then run for it.

But I was in for a surprise. Mrs Bushell, from 1C, was already outside her flat. She was having a flaming row with the little ginger-haired man from 1D. The little ginger-haired man was complaining that Mrs Bushell's music had kept him up all night.

'Don't think I don't know why you're doing it,' said the little ginger-haired man. 'It's because you don't like my dog!'

I posted Dad's letter quietly into a rubbish-bin, and crept

back to our flat. Luckily Dad had fallen asleep, still on the lounge carpet. I volunteered to take the day off school, so I could man the stereo. Mum got really annoyed and threw my briefcase at me. The pop music was turning her into a hooligan, just like Dad said it would.

Nigel and I put on our biggest winning smiles, and set off for school past 1C. We hummed our Beethoven and put our hands round our ears, to make sure the country-and-western music couldn't brainwash us. We thought we were safe when we reached 1D, but there was another surprise coming. Jazz music was blasting through 1D's window. It was as loud as Elvis, Beethoven and Dolly Parton all rolled into one. The little ginger-haired man was standing at his door, with one fist raised, and his doggy under his other arm.

'Good morning!' I shouted.

'*What?*' he shouted back.

It was a strange kind of day at school. Things seemed too quiet. After a while, the music war began to seem like a dream. Dad said that it was like that at the start of the Second World War. The sun was shining, the birds were twittering, and all kinds of normal things were going on. It was hard to imagine that tanks were rumbling, or shells were booming, or Elvis Parsley was coming on for the nine thousandth time.

We set off home, as usual, at three-thirty. Nigel lumbered along under the weight of my briefcase and satchel and extra overcoat, moaning, as usual.

But half-way back we noticed an unusual rumbling sound, like a huge jet engine taking off. You couldn't say whether the sound was high, or low, or thin, or fat. It was pure noise, and it was getting louder the closer we got to home.

As we turned into our road, we realized what the noise was. Every single flat, for a quarter of a mile, had their stereo on, all turned to maximum. The music of the world was blending together to make one enormous great fart. A police car was stopped outside one of the flats, and a man in a suit was arguing furiously with the policemen. At least, I thought he was arguing, because I could see his arms waving about.

To our horror, the police jumped back in their car, and pulled up beside me and Nigel.

'Which way is 1B?' they demanded.

'That way!' I said, pointing in the opposite direction to our house.

The police sped off. So did we. We arrived panting back in our flat, to find Dad on a chair, madly conducting Beethoven with a wooden spoon.

'Now we've seen who's got staying power!' he yelled. 'Now we've seen who's scared of whom!'

'Dad,' I said, tugging at his sock. 'The police are coming.'

Dad stopped conducting. 'The police?' he said. 'Here?'

'Yeah, but you're not scared of them, are you, Dad?' said Nigel. 'You're not scared of anybody!'

Dad's face had gone quite white. He got off the chair. 'Geoffrey,' he said. 'Get the suitcases.'

'It's all right, Dad. I gave them the wrong directions.'

'Get the cases! Don't argue!'

Dad was always saying what was wrong with the police, and I was very surprised he wasn't going to take the chance to tell them personally. Still, I did as I was told, and we rather messily packed a few things. Mum and Dad had a brief debate about leaving the cat, then we formed up into a troupe and stood by the front door. Dad gave us a little lecture, and explained that there was no shame in making a 'tactical retreat'. Then we flung open the front door and marched out smartly in single file.

The police car still hadn't found our flat. But there before us was a black taxi. Who should be stepping out of this taxi but Sonia, our friend and neighbour. She looked relaxed and happy and had a deep brown tan.

'Hello, Mr and Mrs Farmer,' she said brightly. 'Goodness, noisy today, isn't it?'

Sonia told us all about her wonderful weekend in Paris, while Mum and Dad stood with their mouths open.

'Oh no,' she said, as she opened the front door. 'I didn't leave my stereo on, did I?'

Sonia explained all about her stereo, and how it automatically played the record again once it had finished.

'I really am so sorry,' she said. 'It hasn't caused you any trouble, has it?'

Mum, Nigel and I all looked straight at Dad. For a long while there was no change in his face. Then, slowly, a little smile crept on to his lips.

'Oh no,' he said. 'No trouble at all.'

Teeth

JAN MARK

Eric still lives in the town where we grew up. He says he wants to stay close to his roots. That's a good one. You can say that again. Roots.

Some people are rich because they are famous. Some people are famous just for being rich. Eric Donnelly is one of the second sort, but I knew him before he was either, when we were at Victoria Road Primary together. I don't really *know* Eric any more, but I can read about him in the papers any time, same as you can. He was in one of the colour supplements last Sunday, with a photograph of his house all over a double-page spread. You need a double-page spread to take in Eric these days. He was being interviewed about the things he really considers important in life, which include, in the following order, world peace, conservation, foreign travel (to promote world peace, of course, not for *fun*), his samoyeds (a kind of very fluffy wolf) and his wife. He didn't mention money but anyone who has ever known Eric – for three years like I did or even for five minutes – knows that on Eric's list it comes at the top, way in front of world peace. In the photo he was standing with the wife and three of the samoyeds in front of the house, trying to look ordinary. To *prove* how ordinary he is he was explaining how he used to be very poor and clawed his way up using only his own initiative. Well, that's true as far as it goes: his own initiative and his own claws – and other people's teeth. He didn't mention the teeth.

'Well,' says Eric modestly, in the Sunday supplement, 'it's a standing joke, how I got started. Cast-iron baths.' That too is true as far as it goes. When Eric was fifteen he got a job with one of those firms that specialize in house clearances. One day they cleared a warehouse which happened to contain two hundred and fifty Victorian cast-iron baths with claw feet. It occurred to Eric that there were a lot of people daft enough to actually *want* a Victorian bath with claw feet; people, that is, who hadn't had to grow up with them, so he bought the lot at a knock-down price, did them up and flogged them. That bit's well known, but in the Sunday supplement he decided to come clean. He came clean about how he'd saved enough money to buy the baths in the first place by collecting scrap metal, cast-offs, old furniture and returnable bottles. 'A kind of rag-and-bone man,' said Eric, with the confidence of a tycoon who can afford to admit that he used to be a rag-and-bone man because he isn't one any more. He still didn't mention the teeth.

I first met Eric Donnelly in the Odeon one Saturday morning during the kid's show. I'd seen him around at school before – he was in the year above mine – but here he was sitting next to me. I was trying to work out one of my front teeth which had been loose for ages and was now hanging by a thread. I could open and shut it, like a door, but it kept getting stuck and I'd panic in case it wouldn't go right side round again. In the middle of the millionth episode of *Thunder Riders* it finally came unstuck and shot out. I just managed to field it and after having a quick look I shoved it in my pocket. Eric leaned over and said in my earhole, 'What are you going to do with that, then?'

'Put it under me pillow,' I said. 'Me mum'll give me sixpence for it.'

'Oh, the tooth fairy,' said Eric. I hadn't quite liked to mention the tooth fairy. I was only eight but I knew already what happened to lads who went round talking about fairies.

'Give it to us, then,' Eric said. 'I'll pay you sixpence.'

'Do you collect them?' I asked him.

'Sort of,' said Eric. 'Go on – sixpence. What about it?'

'But me mum knows it's loose,' I said.

'Sevenpence, then.'

'She'll want to know where it went.'

'Tell her you swallowed it,' Eric said. 'She won't care.'

He was right, and I didn't care either, although I cared a lot about the extra penny. You might not believe this, but a penny – an old penny – was worth something then, that is, you noticed the difference between having it and not having it. I've seen my own kids lose a pound and not think about it as much as I thought about that extra penny. Eric was already holding it out on his palm in the flickering darkness – one penny and two threepenny bits. I took them and gave him the tooth in a hurry – I didn't want to miss any more of *Thunder Riders*.

'Your tooth's gone, then,' my mum said, when I came home and she saw the gap.

'I swallowed it,' I said, looking sad. 'Never mind,' she said, and I could see she was relieved that the tooth fairy hadn't got to fork out another sixpence. I'd lost two teeth the week before. They started coming out late but once they got going there was no holding them and my big brother Ted was still shedding the odd grinder. She gave me a penny, as a sort of consolation prize, so I was tuppence up on that tooth. I didn't tell her about flogging it to Eric Donnelly for sevenpence. She'd have thought it was a bit odd. I thought it was a bit odd myself.

It was half-term that weekend so I didn't see Eric till we were back at school on Wednesday. Yes, Wednesday. Half-terms were short, then, like everything else: trousers, money ... He was round the back of the bog with Brian Ferris.

'Listen,' Eric was saying, 'threepence, then.'

'Nah,' said Brian, 'I want to keep it.'

'But you said your mum didn't believe in the tooth fairy,' Eric persisted. 'You been losing teeth for two years for *nothing*! If you let me have it you'll get threepence – *four*pence.'

'I want it,' said Brian. 'I want to keep it in a box and watch it go rotten.'

'Fivepence,' said Eric.

'It's mine. I want it.' Brian walked away and Eric retired defeated, but at dinner time I caught him at it again with Mary Arnold, over by the railings.

'How much does your tooth fairy give you?' he asked.

'A shilling,' said Mary, smugly.

'No deal, then,' Eric said, shrugging.

'But I'll let *you* have it for thixpenth,' said Mary, and smiled coyly. She always was soft, that Mary.

I started to keep an eye on Eric after that, him and his collection. It wasn't *what* he was collecting that was strange – Tony Mulholland collected bottle tops – it was the fact that he was prepared to pay. I noticed several things. First, the size of the tooth had nothing to do with the amount that Eric would cough up. A socking great molar might go for a penny, while a little worn-down bottom incisor would change hands at sixpence or sevenpence. Also, that he would never go above elevenpence. That was his ceiling. No one ever got a shilling out of Eric Donnelly, even for a great big thing with roots. Charlie McEvoy had one pulled by the dentist and brought it to school for Eric but Eric only gave him sevenpence for it.

'Here, Charlie,' I said, at break. 'What's he do with them?'

'Search me,' said Charlie, 'he's had three of mine.'

'D'you have a tooth fairy at home?' I was beginning to smell a rat.

'Yes,' said Charlie. 'Let's go and beat up Ferris.' He was a hard man, was McEvoy; started early. He's doing ten years for GBH right now, and the Mulhollands are waiting for him when he comes out.

'No – hang about. How much?'

'Sixpence.' I was quite surprised. I wouldn't have put it past old McEvoy to keep a blunt instrument under the pillow, bean the tooth fairy and swipe the night's takings. He was a big fellow, even at eight. I wasn't quite so big, but Eric, although he was a year older, was smaller than me. That day I followed him home.

It was not easy to follow Eric home. They tended to marry early in that family so Eric not only had a full set of grandparents but also two great-grandmothers and enough aunties to upset the national average. As his mum seemed to have a baby about every six months Eric was always going to stay with one of them or another. He was heading for one of his great-grandmas that evening, along Jubilee Crescent. I nailed him down by the phone box.

'Listen, Donnelly,' I said. 'What are you doing with all them teeth?'

Give him credit, he didn't turn a hair. A lot of kids would have got scared, but not Eric. He just said, 'You got one for me, then?'

'Well, no,' I said, 'but I might have by Saturday.'

'Sevenpence?' said Eric, remembering the previous trans-action, I suppose. He had a head for figures.

'Maybe,' I said, 'but I want to know what you do with them.'

'What if I won't tell you?' Eric said.

'I'll knock all yours out,' I suggested, so he told me. As I thought, it was all down to the grannies and aunties. They were sorry for poor little Eric – Dad out of work, all those brothers and sisters and no pocket money. If he lost a tooth while he was staying with one of them he put it under the pillow and the tooth fairy paid up. There being two great-grannies, two grannies and seven aunties, it was hard for anyone to keep tabs on the number of teeth Eric lost and it hadn't taken him long to work out that if he didn't over-do things he could keep his eleven tooth fairies in business for years. Kids who didn't have a tooth fairy of their own were happy to flog him a fang for a penny. If he had to pay more than sixpence the tooth went to Great-Granny Ennis, who had more potatoes than the rest of them put together.

By the time that he was eleven I calculate that Eric Don-nelly had lost one hundred teeth, which is approximately twice as many as most of us manage to lose in a lifetime. With the money he saved he bought a second-hand barrow and toured the streets touting for scrap, returnable bottles and so on, which was what earned him enough to buy the two hundred and fifty Victorian baths with claw feet which is the beginning of the public part of Eric's success story, where we came in. I suppose there is some justice in the fact that at thirty-eight Eric no longer has a single tooth he can call his own.

No – I am not Eric's dentist. I am his dustman, and I sometimes catch a glimpse of the old cushion grips as I empty the bin. Occasionally I turn up just as Eric is leaving for a board meeting. He flashes his dentures at me in a nervous grin and I give him a cheery wave like honest dustmen are meant to do.

'Morning, Donnelly,' I shout merrily. 'Bought any good teeth lately?' He hates that.

The Rescue of Karen Arscott

GENE KEMP

Amongst us lot she stuck out like a sore thumb. Or rather an orchid on a rubbish tip. Not that I know what an orchid looks like but you get the idea. She first appeared at our Wednesday morning Assembly, stuck there in line between Lindy Brown and Karen Arscott and there couldn't have been any place to do more for her – talk about a rose between two thorns. Lindy is knee high to a corgi, but thin with it, pipe cleaner shape, with a drippy nose and straggly hair. Her main hobby is weeping in corners. Mrs Conway, that's our class teacher, keeps leading us aside in turn, asking us to be *kind*, telling us to try to get her to join in. Poor Lindy had problems, she says, who doesn't, asks my friend Angie, rolling her big eyes.

Now Karen is different. Worse. Worse than anything you can imagine. She looks like that creature from the Black Lagoon, or out of the depths of the Id or whatever it was in those old movies. Get out of my way, she snarls. So I do. We all do. I've been getting out of her way for the past ten years since she flattened me in the Infants' playground and took my lunch and my new pencil case. Next day I brought my mum into the playground. After she'd gone, Karen flattened me again. After that I gave up saying anything about Karen – just learnt to move very fast in the opposite direction whenever I saw her. And the boys learnt to move even faster. On one of her bad days she could clear the playground quicker than the school dentist arriving. When we left the Primary we hoped she'd go to a different Comprehensive. We kept saying all the good things we knew about the others very loudly when she was about. But it was hopeless, as we realized when we heard her mum telling our teacher that Karen didn't want to leave her form mates. Her mum looked like Giant Haystacks, the wrestler, so our teacher agreed, nodding up and down a lot.

But practice had made me very nippy, and there was a good crowd of us – Angie, Tamsin, Jackie and Pat. So we managed without too much aggro even when she turned up in our class despite there being four streams to each year.

No, the one who copped it was Lindy, fresh from another school and born loser from the start. We did try to stop it, to help, but Lindy was so wet and Karen so tough that by our year it was more or less the thing that those two paired off and Karen was The Boss.

And then, there in the hall one gloomy February morning stood this girl in between the two of them. And she was beautiful. Her hair was long and black, her face was pale, her eyes misty. Even Angie looked ordinary beside her. The rest of us like Rejects United.

Back in the classroom everyone crowded round her as they always do with anyone new till the novelty wears off. I tried to join in but there was no room so I thought I might just as well get on with the homework I hadn't finished the night before. Then I made out a beauty programme wondering if Mum would let me dye my hair. It would be smashing not to be a natural born mouse, and to be slim. Not that I'm really very fat, and a thirty-six bra sounds all right except if you're only five foot tall you look more as if you're wearing a bolster than the Dawson Comprehensive answer to Miss

THE RESCUE OF KAREN ARSCOTT

World. Then I chucked the list away. Why bother? Never, never in a million light years was I going to look like that new girl. What was her name? Harriet, Mrs Conway was saying, Harriet Carter. Just look at Darren Carr making shapes with his hands in the air. He would, the cheeky so-and-so.

'Lisa, pay attention, please. Lisa!'

I sat up. 'Yes Miss.'

Back to basics.

She turned out to be a very quiet girl. Her work was good and she didn't put a foot wrong with the teachers or anyone, being friendly to everyone but not too friendly and going straight home after school. She seemed to live some distance away, no one knew where. In fact Harriet was a bit of a mystery, and rumours soon ran round the school that a) she was a South American millionairess in hiding because of kidnapping threats, b) she was a refugee from Eastern Europe, c) her mother was dead and she had to get home to cook for her dad. Somehow the last seemed the most likely. So, said Angie, she's got problems, too.

In the end she just became another one of the class. The boys gave up chasing her when they saw she really wasn't interested, and focus switched back to Angie who was now going out with the captain of the soccer team, who (they said) had never been out with a girl before. What will she make of him, we wondered. Also, we were doing a bit of work, since the teachers mostly came in saying, There's only so many weeks left now till the exams, filling us with terror – well some of us.

It was a very wet spring term. Every day it rained. Karen developed boils on her face which didn't do much for her looks and even less for her temper. Lindy actually appeared in new PE kit. Miss Johnson had gone on at her so much I suppose she was driven to it. Karen threw it down the loo so that it was soaking wet for the lesson. For once Lindy complained and for once we backed her, and Karen caught it in the neck, detentions for a week, etc. But Lindy appeared with a bruise on her face. Walked into a door she said quietly, my own silly fault, I ought to wear my glasses.

We stayed indoors at lunch-time, it was always so wet, and we had access to the library, to the hall for badminton, and to other rooms for things like chess, stamp club and so on. I went to the Art Room, where I was painting Harriet. I'd asked if I could for my Art continuous assessment.

'Might be a good idea,' said old Hamby, grinning. He's a joker, that guy. 'Your work's jolly good, Lisa,' I started to beam like the Cheshire Cat, 'but there isn't enough of it, haha.' And he went away chuckling to himself.

'Some people are getting senile,' I said. So I painted Harriet. I got to know her face well, but what went on behind it was still a mystery.

Someone who also came to the Art Room was Lindy. And without Karen who was forbidden to go in there because she'd wrecked it on three occasions.

This day we came out together, Harriet, Lindy and me, and Lindy was quite pink and human and chatty. Her leaf and tree prints were really good and she was always better when she was doing something arty, seemed to have more confidence. Besides, Harriet, though she hardly said anything herself, always got Lindy to chat away merrily.

Karen Arscott sat in the middle of the corridor blocking the way to the classroom. Lindy turned pale, the bruise on her face showing up clearly.

'Whatcher bin doing, then?' said Karen to Lindy.

Without a word Lindy handed over her folder.

'Load o' crap, ain't it?' said Karen and threw Lindy's collection on the floor and stamped on it.

'Any objections?' she went on.

Like a shadow Harriet slipped between her and Lindy, pushed Karen back on to the chair then tipped the chair and Karen up. A bellow of rage echoed down the corridor as Karen lumbered to her feet. A crowd gathered. They were all coming but no one was going to interfere, least of all the boys, though cries of, 'Let her have it, Harriet,' were heard. Karen charged at Harriet, who waited almost carelessly till the last possible minute, then moved to one side, and Karen crashed heavily into the wall, the picture on the rail above descending on to her head and putting paid to her. A cheer went up. Until,

'Just what is going on here?' said Mr Keithley, the Head-master.

But Lindy went on her knees beside Karen and lifted her head on to her lap. Harriet, paler than ever, looked at them, then turned and walked through the crowd, who just melted away before her.

I never saw her again.

Mr Keithley, who always seemed to know everything that went on in the school, said Karen had got her deserts at last, and would we please pack up Harriet's things for her as she would be moving on. So we did. Lindy looked after Karen like a mother hen with its chick, and there was no more trouble in that direction. Karen was a changed person. She depended on Lindy a lot.

The weather improved. The sun shone at last. After a time I stopped resenting the dullness of school without Harriet. And, after a longer time, I forgot her and to my surprise found a boyfriend. The portrait? Well, I kept that, though I didn't hand it in for assessment. For one thing it wasn't finished. Besides, I didn't want people looking at it and marking it B or C or lower.

About three years later I went to Art School, and moved my gear into a bedsit for term time. As I was clearing out a drawer, a photo in the old newspaper-lining caught my eye, I don't know why. I looked more closely and saw that it resembled Harriet. But an older Harriet with shorter hair. I realized it was her mother.

Underneath the caption read: Mrs Adrienne Carter was today convicted of the manslaughter of her husband, Frederick Herbert Carter. She attacked and killed him with a heavy stick after he had severely beaten their daughter, Harriet, aged nine years.

Oh, Harriet, Harriet.

Pictures

TOBY FORWARD

The teacher looked at Amina's painting. 'It's lovely dear. It's so nice I think your parents would like to see it. You can take yours home as a special treat.'

Amina was disappointed; she wanted her picture on the wall with all the others. It didn't look any better to her than theirs did. She knew it was better than the ones with smudged faces and arms and legs that didn't seem to belong to the body, but it wasn't as nice as the very pretty one with the blue dress for Mary, and the light shining around Babyjesus's head. It was all a puzzle, but she was often puzzled.

'Shall I put it on the wall first, and take it home when they come down?'

The teacher frowned and thought for a while. 'Perhaps it'll get dusty and fade,' she decided. 'You want your mummy and daddy to see it at its best.'

Amina nodded, a sign of defeat rather than conviction and put the drying picture on her desk, ready to go into her bag at the end of the day. The white faces of twenty-four Marys looked down pityingly on the brown face of Amina's picture.

She put the picture on the table in the room at the back of the shop where she lived and smoothed out the creases. It made a cheerful display in the dingy room. In one corner the television was on; piled in corners were cardboard boxes of sweets and crisps, washing-up liquid and soap, tinned fruit and little bottles of spices. The stockroom of the shop was too small to hold all the different lines that her father needed to carry to make a profit from his long opening hours and local trade. Always there was a slight sense, not entirely in the nose, of food smells and cheap unguents. These combined, rather than counteracted one another, so that all Amina's clothes carried with them a suggestion of this room. She had never known why people drew away from her a little on buses and in lifts. It was not always through residual dislike of her colour, but often because she smelled. Piles of washing waiting to be ironed, drew in the atmosphere of the room and made it her aura.

Amina set about tidying a little space for herself so that she could settle to wait for her mother. She wanted to ask where they could display the picture. She hoped it could go over the gas fire. The television glowed indiscreetly in the corner and captured her mind. She sank into her chair and became absorbed in the invaders from space, the petty quizzes, cartoon chases, and finally the military music which announced the news. Little of this made any impression on her memory or her beliefs.

Her mother came in the room for a rest before serving in the shop for another three hours till nine o'clock. She was a thin woman who had spread in the middle. Her legs showed the slim girl she had once been and her ankles seemed too fragile to support the fat belly that rested high above them. When she saw Amina, the tiredness fell from her face, and the impatience, layered on by dealing all day with customers, dropped away. A smile plucked at the corners of her mouth and she spread her arms. Amina popped out of her chair like a cork from a toy gun and landed in her mother's arms. There was an intimacy between them that came from the knowledge that there would be no more children for her. Amina was the daughter of her parents' middle age. Their family was thought to be long over when she announced her intention of joining it.

The sharp contours of the little girl's body made comfortable hollows in her mother's soft flesh. They stood for some seconds, holding one another. Amina wriggled to free herself.

'Look.'

Mrs Iqbal smiled and waited for her gift. Amina reached toward the picture. The smile went from her mother's face as quickly as the tiredness and irritation had faded a few moments earlier.

'What is this?'

She never snapped at Amina, but the tone of interrogation was unfamiliar enough to the girl to cause her some anxiety. She did not want to anger her mother.

'The teacher sent it home.'

'Why? Is it not for school? Is it not good?'

Amina was near to tears. 'It is very good. Teacher says it is too good to spoil on the wall at the school. She sent it for you.'

Mrs Iqbal struggled to keep the emotion from her voice. She took the picture and folded it, first in half, then quarters, each time with a swift and neat crease. Then, she tore it across. The pieces were pushed into a bin. Amina squealed as she saw the destruction of her beautiful picture; but her mother took her arm, pulled her slowly but firmly to her, and sank to a chair, settling the girl on her lap. She pulled Amina's head down so that it rested on her experienced bosom and talked quietly to her.

'Who is in this picture?' she murmured.

'Babyjesus and Mary.'

'Why do you draw them?'

61

'Soon it will be Christmas, when Babyjesus came to save us.'

Mrs Iqbal felt her head tighten inside, but her questions remained quiet.

'What is this story?'

Amina told her mother how the angel had spoken to Mary, of the journey to Bethlehem, the shepherds, the kings, the death of all the baby boys, and the miraculous escape to Egypt. She loved the story. She told her mother of the pictures they had drawn of Mary and Jesus, the frieze that they would paint, the little Christmas cards that they were going to bring home, and the play that all the parents would come to school to see.

When the story was over, Mrs Iqbal waited for a few moments until Amina was still and comfortable again. Then she explained. 'You must never let your father know this,' she said. 'We do not draw pictures, especially not the Prophet from Nazareth and his mother.'

Gently she explained that the Prophet Muhammad had forbidden the drawing of the Prophet from Nazareth and his mother, in case they should be worshipped. She told Amina what a good and holy man Jesus of Nazareth was and how his mother was a great and holy lady, but that, for Muslims, they should not be spoken of as they were in the school.

That evening, Mrs Iqbal told her husband that she could not work in the shop, that Amina needed her. It was not good for the girl to be alone every night with only the television. All evening mother and daughter sat happily drawing together. Mrs Iqbal brought in a new box of coloured pencils from the shop, ignoring her husband's grumbles about expense. She and Amina drew and traced many beautiful patterns on gleaming sheets of white paper: lovely patterns, swirls and angles, colours and whorls, they darted in and out like small animals chasing one another through complicated passageways. They followed slow, sensuous curves, like young lovers courting one another through the elaborate ritual of a rigid but harmonious society. But there were no people.

Mrs Iqbal took the Qur'ān from its shelf. With unfeigned devotion, she gently turned its pages, showing Amina the subtle and gracious designs which illuminated the sacred text. As they sat and worked and talked together the bond of intimacy reformed between them and when she kissed her mother goodnight Amina was relaxed and happy.

At school, Amina drew her Christmas card. The same patterns that her mother had taught her took the place of the crib, with the oxen and asses. No wise men or shepherds interrupted the lively and sinuous decoration of her pencils. Her teacher was bewildered.

'This is not right. You should be drawing the stable.'

Amina was courteous but firm in her answer. 'I do not draw stables. I draw patterns.'

The teacher fetched her a new sheet of card and folded it double. 'Here you are, dear. Do another of your nice drawings of Mary and Jesus.'

Amina was surprised. Why did the teacher not understand her explanation? 'I do not draw people.'

'Of course you do. You draw lovely people. Just because we didn't put your last picture on the wall doesn't mean you can't do well.'

'I know. The last picture was too good to put on the wall.'

The teacher blushed as she remembered the lie.

'But, I do not draw people.'

The teacher determined to make up for her mistake in rejecting the picture. 'Now look, Amina, that was a lovely picture, and I wish now I hadn't let you take it home. It means that we haven't been able to see your work on our walls.' She spoke in a bright and encouraging voice, that Amina had not heard her use before.

'Here is a nice new piece of card and here is a sheet of paper. Draw the same picture on both, dear, and paint it, then you can take the card home, and we'll put the picture on the wall.'

Mechanically, she bared her teeth in a smile and walked away before Amina could explain again that she did not draw people.

For the next hour, as she worked, the white faces of Mary and Jesus smiled down from the walls at her. Slowly the pictures took shape. The paper and card were filled with the forms from the myth. Amina enjoyed the work and she had a delicate touch. By the end of the day, she could sit back in her desk and see the completed pattern, the Christmas card with its animals and Holy Family and the picture for the wall, a traditional, if slightly dusky Madonna.

The teacher smiled in genuine pleasure when she saw the finished work. 'See, dear. You're very good.' For the first time, she really examined the picture, ignoring the disturbing colouring of the features. 'Very good,' she said. She pushed the card into Amina's hand and whisked away the patterned card and the picture.

'Home time.'

That night, Amina sat alone as usual in front of the television. Her mother and father worked together in the shop, taking time only to put her to bed. The street light outside filtered in through her thin curtains and picked out the little bunches of flowers that dotted the paper on her walls. Half a mile away, in school, a brown-faced Mary smiled unceasingly down at a bin in the corner of the room. On the top of the bin was a folded piece of card with an accurate and lovingly-reproduced illumination from the Qur'ān. Below Amina's bedroom, in the shop, Mr and Mrs Iqbal sold Christmas cards, men's magazines, fairy lights and crackers. In the litter bin, fixed to the street light that forced light in through the curtains of the little girl's room, lay a card, skilfully and lovingly produced at school that day. Amina had kept it in her hand all the way home, looking at it sometimes and asking the face on it what she should do.

In the end she had dropped it into the bin before pushing open the door of the shop and hearing the jingle of the bell as she entered. Rain soaked the card. The paint ran down, and the stiffness relaxed into limp decay. The Mother of God cradled her son in her arms, in amongst the orange peelings and sweet wrappings.

Gypsy

SAM McBRATNEY

Gypsy came into the house before Danny Murray was born. She hung on the wall above the battered old piano with the yellow keys. Danny didn't like her cross face when he was little. Sometimes when he did his piano practice he climbed up on the stool and turned the picture to the wall so that she couldn't listen.

Gypsy had thin red lips under a crooked big nose and her eyelids were always half-closed in a sly sort of way – as if to hide what she was really thinking. The pearls round her neck looked like blobs of paint from close up, but when you stepped back they caught the light, and glowed. Like magic, really. Gypsy was so real that Danny used to wonder whether she was still alive somewhere in the world.

One day Catherine Parr from down the street came into the house and she said that Gypsy's lips were red because she ate poison berries. She stuck out her tongue at Gypsy and she made Danny do the same.

When Danny was nine Gypsy got him into trouble. He climbed up on the piano stool and tried to give her a shave with his daddy's razor and wobbling brush, but his mother came into the room at the wrong moment, and caught him in the act.

'Oh my glory!' she said. Mountains of creamy lather stood out from Gypsy's chin like snow-capped mountains on a map

66

of the world. An avalanche of snow had blocked up her long, roman nose. 'Danny Murray! Oh, I will murder you, you bad article. Brian – come you in here this minute, he's shaving *Gypsy*!'

His daddy arrived, breathless, and did some staring at Gypsy's altered face.

'What are you playing at? Are you stupid? The only thing in the house that could be worth a fortune, and what do *you* do with it? Give it a blasted *shave*!'

And so Danny found himself driven up the stairs by the flat of his father's hand. That was the first time he realized that Gypsy might not be just any old picture. In some mysterious way, maybe she was worth something.

About this time Dr Moore began to call at the house to examine Danny's father, who wasn't feeling well. During one of these visits the doctor happened to notice Gypsy.

'Mrs Murray,' he said, peering through his bushy eyebrows, 'I have to remark on that dark-skinned beauty on your wall. Now that's what I call a proper picture! Where did you get her – did you pick her up cheap at one of the auctions?'

'No, sure we've had that for years,' said Danny's mother. 'Maggie O'Brien and her man lit out for Canada and they auctioned all their stuff at the front door. My grandfather bought the picture and her mangle for two and six.'

Dr Moore smiled, and repeated 'Two and six!' as he turned the painting over in his hands. 'Pity it's not signed. But look at this canvas, I'd say it wasn't done by one of your weekend artists. Did you ever think of selling her?'

'Ah no,' said his mother, turning a bit red. 'Brian says we couldn't sell our luck.'

'Well now – give me the first refusal,' said Dr Moore, who aimed a massive wink at Danny as he put his stethoscope on

Gypsy's chest and pretended to be deafened by the noise of her insides.

After that Danny's parents talked about Gypsy as if she was money in the bank. His daddy used to say that he was going to sell Gypsy and buy a yacht and keep it in the harbour at Ballyholme. His mother wanted a house in the country with chickens and a goat. 'How Will We Spend Gypsy' became a favourite family game. Then, when Danny turned eleven, his father died, and of course everything changed.

The Headmaster said special prayers for Danny in Assembly one morning. People were sorry for him because his daddy had gone away to heaven, and indeed, he was sorry for himself and for his mummy. It was a long time before she did many of her ordinary things about the house, such as play the old piano in the living-room. Then one day she played and made Danny sing that stupid song about Paddy McGinty's goat, and Danny felt good. They bought a black labrador pup and they had trouble teaching it not to widdle everywhere.

Danny noticed another change that came over his life at this time: there was no money to spend now that they had to live on what his mummy earned. Sometimes he remembered the day when he bought three bars of Caramilk in the sweetie shop and ate them one after another on the way to school.

'You are one greedy spoiled pig, Danny Murray,' Catherine Parr had told him, just because he only gave her two squares.

Now, times had changed. Catherine Parr was able to go on the school trip to Brittany, but Danny's mother sat down and cried when he told her what it would cost. Even when she became Manageress of the laundry where she worked on the Newtonards Road, still she complained that he grew too fast and ranted about the awful things he could do to a pair of shoes.

'I am going to buy you a pair of wooden Dutch clogs, Danny Murray,' she used to say.

His mother was very friendly with the woman who owned the local fruit, vegetable and flower shop. This lady, Miss Finlay, gave Danny a job after school on Fridays and all day Saturdays. He spent most of the time sweeping the floors and making up delivery boxes. One afternoon Danny was wrapping an old newspaper round six big earthy leeks when an interesting headline caught his eye:

FORTUNE IN THE ATTIC

A County Antrim farmer learned yesterday that the painting found in his attic could be worth as much as £80,000.

'I'm only flabbergasted,' he told our reporter. 'It's been up there for years, I nearly threw it out. I don't even like it, you know – I like pictures with horses in them.'

When asked what he was going to do with his windfall, Mr Cowan said, 'Enjoy it!'

Danny began to think. If his mummy had £80,000 she wouldn't have to scrimp and save or worry about the price of shoes. He thought of Gypsy's sly, hooded eyes; of the fine, strong jaw he'd once tried to shave; of the pearls round her neck and how they seemed to glow from within if the light was right. Only a good artist could paint like that, even Dr Moore had said so.

How much, he wondered, was Gypsy really worth?

'Daniel Murray,' called Miss Finlay from the front of the shop, 'what's keeping those leeks – are you growing them, or what?'

That very evening, Danny made a point of sitting with his mother while she did some ironing. From time to time she wet the clothes with vapour from a plastic spray.

'Mummy.'

'U-huh?'

'Miss Finlay says if you take a picture into a shop near the City Hall, they'll tell you what it's worth.'

'Is that a fact, Danny.'

'What would you buy if we sold Gypsy?'

For a moment or two, no answer came. His mother squeezed a squirt of misty water over the collar of a shirt.

'I couldn't sell Gypsy, I've had her since I was a wee girl.'

'But if you *did* sell her, what would you buy?'

'A cuckoo clock!' said his mother, aiming a squirt of water at him. 'Now run away out and play.'

Two more weeks went by, bringing the end of term and the start of the Easter holidays. Danny was bored in the house on his own. Most of his best friends were away with the school to Brittany and it didn't help him to think what a great time they must all be having over there. One Tuesday afternoon he came back from walking the dog in the Ormeau Park, and made a decision that set his blood racing.

He gently lifted Gypsy from the wall, put her into a large carrier bag, and caught a bus into town.

The journey into the centre of Belfast seemed to take about two minutes, for Danny's mind would not be still when he thought of what might happen in the next half hour. Goodbye Mr Scrimp and Mr Save. His mother might even give up her job! They could both fly out to see Uncle Robert in New Zealand or buy a house in the country and keep chickens and a car. Danny could think of dozens of ways of spending Gypsy, even if she wasn't worth quite as much as 80,000 pounds.

He walked down Wellington Place and stood outside the shop with his heart beating like an engine, urging him on. His blood quickened, but his mind refused to be driven and he could not move. His mother would have a fit if she saw him right now! Danny closed his eyes and swallowed, thinking nervously how this was a bit like getting into the cold sea at Millisle. He took the plunge and went right in.

He was the only customer in the cool and very quiet gallery. The central area of the shop was fairly dim compared with the walls, which were illuminated by strips of fluorescent lighting. Some of the pictures hanging there were so huge that they made Gypsy look like a puny little thing – and to his amazement, Danny saw some very fancy carpets hanging on the walls. 'Funny place to keep your carpets,' he was thinking when a voice spoke.

'Yes? What do you want?'

The man who now approached wore a shabby Aran jumper. Using his fingers as a rake, he shifted his long grey hair away from his face.

'I've got a picture here,' said Danny. 'Could you tell me please if it's worth anything?'

'Another one. All right, let's take a look at it.'

The man fitted glasses over his nose as he carried Gypsy a little closer to the window. He tapped the canvas with his fingernail and turned her over to examine the back just as Dr Moore had done all those years ago. Danny wanted to tell him some interesting things about his picture – how her name was Gypsy, that they'd had her for years and years, how she was supposed to be lucky – but he didn't have time. The man whipped the glasses off his face.

'This painting has no commercial value whatsoever. The frame itself might fetch a penny or two if it was competently restored, but the work itself . . . ? Most likely a student's copy. No.'

Danny accepted back his picture without speaking. No commercial value. A copy. That final word fell on his ears like a blow – No. He swallowed hard, gathering his courage, wanting to strike back.

'But . . . didn't you see her pearls?'

'I saw her pearls.'

Gypsy. How it destroyed him to think she wasn't even worth a cuckoo clock.

'But how do you *know*? How do you know she isn't worth anything?'

'Look, son,' said the man, 'what's your name?'

'Danny Murray.'

'Right. Suppose that twenty or thirty women lined up outside this shop and one of them was your mother. And they all shouted, 'Danny Murray' one after another. Do you think you'd know your mother's voice, could you pick it out from the others?'

'Probably.'

'Well that's how it is with paintings. You know your mother's voice when you hear it because you're an expert on that topic. A great and valuable painting is like an old friend – an expert like me can pick it out immediately. Now go home, and take that Gypsy with you. A painting doesn't have to be worth money to be valuable.'

Away he went into a far corner of his shop, leaving Danny

to shove Gypsy into the carrier bag any old way, as if he was ashamed of her now that she was just plain cheap, and angry with her for making a fool out of him.

I hate that man! he thought as he crossed the road at Bedford Street lights, I hate him and his stupid shop and I hate his stupid carpets on his stupid walls.

How Will You Spend Gypsy? The game was over. Perhaps his mother had known all along. And Dr Moore. His daddy, too. Maybe I was the only one who believed in Gypsy, thought Danny. The whole business filled him with such a deep, vague sadness that he wanted to be very, very young again.

When he got home his mother said,

'And where have you been to, my lad! And just be careful what you say because I think I know.'

'Mummy I just took it into that shop.'

'Did you! Well you had no business taking it anywhere, give it to me, here.'

She examined the picture carefully for signs of damage, and seemed satisfied.

'And what did they say in that shop?'

'I didn't go in,' Danny said quickly. 'I hadn't the nerve. Well, it was a big shop.'

All of a sudden his mother giggled, and gave him a peck on the cheek.

'Ah dear love you, sure you're only young.'

She fitted the picture over the lighter patch of wallpaper that marked the spot, and said,

'There you are now, Gypsy,' as if things were more or less back to normal.

The Day We Threw the Switch on Georgie Tozer

BRIAN ALDERSON

George Tozer was one of those clean boys. They're not very common creatures, that's true but you probably know what I mean because they seem to be very evenly spread out. Every school, every block, every estate usually has a specimen: boys with unnaturally clean faces, and hair always cleaving neatly to their scalps. Some – and George was one of them – have even been known voluntarily to go with their mothers to the shops, wearing a tie and gloves, and standing one pace to the rear with a wicker basket.

George Tozer was also a good boy. At school he didn't release small rodents in Morning Assembly like Danny Price used to do, and at home he didn't kick the paintwork or slam doors like that girl Rebecca. But if you ask me, this wasn't because he made great efforts to be good; it was more because he was born that way. He just couldn't help it – and that's not really something to be proud of.

But in a perverse way George Tozer was proud of all this goodness and cleanliness, and that was where the trouble started. You see he'd cultivated a rather demure, dimply smirk, and whenever there was any strife he was liable to grin round at everybody, as much as to say: 'Well, it's not my fault' and that was infuriating. The word would go round 'Get Tozer!', but I must say, that when the time came, he was very good at not being got. Nobody knew a more varied selection of back ways home to escape ambush, and no one was better prepared against practical jokes ('Huh! Butter-milk Soap,' he said one day when he came round to our place for tea, casting aside the stuff we'd got from the Magic Shop that's meant to cover you with slime when you wash with it).

It is my belief that George Tozer enjoyed these pranks. It made every day a kind of April-Fools-Day for him and gave him something to look forward to. It also meant that we were constantly trying to find some ingenious new way of tricking him. So it was, that at the time that I'm telling you about we had a scheme planned that we really thought would strike him to the foundations and drive that dimply grin below surface for a week or two. It was all to do with Jackson's ghost . . .

Now Jackson was my best friend – so it isn't actually his ghost I'm talking about, but the ghost that some people thought he'd got in his house. You see Jackson and his sister Jenny lived in this tall, old decrepit place, which their parents had bought for practically nothing because it was said to be haunted. Years ago a fellow had lived there whose wife had killed herself (hanged herself from the attic ceiling by her own hair, so the rumour had it) and word got about that she kept revisiting the scene of the catastrophe. The estate agents said this gave the house 'historic character' but it took a family like the Jacksons to buy it.

They were far too busy to worry about ghosts. Whenever Mr Jackson was at home he climbed under a car and did things to it with grease guns, and as for Mrs Jackson she was a great one for crafts: pottery-classes one week and pokerwork the next. My friend Jackson was actually more nervous than any of them. He said he'd heard slithery noises and gasps overhead when he'd been in his bedroom making a model aeroplane. But his sister Jenny, who had the pokerwork temperament, said it was nonsense and he'd been watching too many Late Nite Horror Shows!

Anyway, this was our plan for tricking old Georgie Tozer, and we thought it quite a neat one: we'd get him round to the Jacksons' to play one afternoon (not too difficult, since his mum was a friend of my mum and J's mum and they were always trying to bring Georgie's good influence to bear on us), then we decided that we'd get him up to the attic and haunt him.

I was to take him up there under the pretext of having tea, all snug and away from the grown-ups, while the other two were ostensibly going to fetch a trayful of things to eat. But Jackson would in fact go down to the cellar where all the electrical switches were, and Jenny would be installed in the attic, and then, at just the right moment, Jackson would throw the switch and plunge the room in darkness and Jenny would turn into the ghost of the unfortunate lady who hanged herself.

Jenny's actual ghostliness was really rather ghastly. The way we'd worked it out was this: when I brought George into the attic she would be hiding in the far corner behind the chest-of-drawers. When the light went out she would creep on to the top of this chest and peer down at Georgie with a torch shining under her chin. I don't know if you've ever tried this, but if you get the torch in the right place it gives the effect of disembodied features floating in mid-air (very horrid). What's more, Jenny had long hair, seemingly just like the woman in the story. She got hold of one of those torches with colour filters so that she could slide different strips across the bulb and turn herself blood-red or sickly-green in a very unnerving way.

We rehearsed the whole exercise over and over again. Jenny rigged up some cushioned steps on to the chest-of-drawers, so that she could get up there quickly and quietly, and she practised holding the torch so that she could get the angles right by instinct. I might say that the first few times that Jackson and I were the audience we were fairly terrified ourselves. The attic was a big one and, in the dark, you had this sense of not knowing where to go to escape this grisly face with its stringy hair.

Well – the day came for our tea-party, and George Tozer and I went back with the Jacksons from school. It was getting towards Christmas – damp and chilly – and we were glad to flop down in front of the Jacksons' fire when we got in. We played some games and Jenny cheated dreadfully, which drew forth arguments from pernickety old George and made us feel very virtuous about putting the frights on him.

Eventually the time came for the haunting. 'I'll go and see about some tea,' said Jenny, and made off apparently towards the kitchen where Mrs Jackson was, I suppose, cutting sandwiches or baking cakes or something. A couple of minutes later, as arranged, Jackson suggested that we all go upstairs for our private picnic and I shepherded George along while J peeled off 'to help' – or rather to get down the cellar where he could turn off the lights.

Everything had been very carefully timed with watches. We knew that it would take George and me about one minute and forty seconds to get up to the attic and park ourselves in chairs by the radiator, with George strategically placed facing Jenny's chest-of-drawers. Then we were going to leave about another half a minute for me to make some excuse and drift off out of the room where I could hold the door shut in case our victim thought to flee from the terror by night. (This wouldn't be easy though. You try escaping from a ghost in a large, pitch-black unfamiliar room with an assortment of chairs, boxes and cast-off bits of furniture all over the floor.)

The plan worked perfectly. We climbed upstairs to the attic with George apparently accepting that afternoon tea in an attic was only to be expected at the Jacksons. We settled down in the place appointed (I was dreadfully worried that Jenny would gasp or giggle or sneeze behind her chest-of-drawers, but she was as quiet as a dormant ghost ought to be) and then I muttered something about seeing where everyone was, and wandered out of the room.

Just as I closed the door behind me Jackson down in the cellar threw the switch and everything went black. The silence and suddenness of the event was alarming in itself, but I hung on to the door handle and tried to hear what was happening through the keyhole. There was a creak as soon as the light went out, which suggested that George had jumped to his feet, but he didn't seem to be moving about, and he didn't seem to be responding to Jenny who, by now, must have been starting her torch routine. There was nothing.

Then suddenly there was more than we bargained for. There was a shriek of a kind that, in that darkness, seemed to come from some caged monster – piercing, but at the same time sobbing and bubbling. It didn't happen just once. It happened again and again, and I shoved the door open to try and find out what was going on. At the same instant on came the lights again, and I saw poor old George Tozer flat on his back on the floor. He looked as though he was in some sort of fit, twitching and jerking, with his skin all blotchy grey, and white round the bottom of his cheeks. 'The face ...' he kept mumbling, 'the face ... the face ... the face ...'

'Don't be daft, George,' I said, 'it's only Jenny' – looking round to see where she'd got to. And as I did so there was a great commotion on the stairs and in burst Mrs Jackson in a frantic temper. 'What the hell's going on! You had us damn near scald ourselves down there!' And there behind her, white-faced and appalled, straight from the kitchen – where she'd been made to stay and make the tea – was Jenny.

The Empty Schoolroom

PAMELA HANSFORD JOHNSON

My mother and father were in India and I had no aunts, uncles or cousins with whom I could spend my holidays; so I stayed behind in the drab and echoing school to amuse myself as best I could, my only companions the housekeeper, the maid, and Mademoiselle Fournier, who also had nowhere else to go.

Our school was just outside the village of Bellançay, which is in the north of France, four or five kilometres from Rouen. It was a tall, narrow house set upon the top of a hill, bare save for the great sweep of beech trees sheltering the long carriage drive. As I look back some twenty-seven years to my life there, it seems to me that the sun never shone, that the grass was always dun-coloured beneath a dun-coloured sky, and that the vast spaces of the lawns were broken perpetually by the scurry of dry brown leaves licked along by a small, bitter wind. This inaccurate impression remains with me because, I suppose, I was never happy at Bellançay. There were twenty or thirty other girls there – French, German or Swiss; I was the only English girl among them. Madame de Vallon, the headmistress, did not love my nation. She could not forget that she had been born in 1815, the year of defeat. With Mademoiselle Maury, the young assistant teacher, I was a little more at ease, for she, even if she did not care for me, had too volatile a nature not to smile and laugh sometimes, even for the benefit of those who were not her favourites.

Mademoiselle Fournier was a dependent cousin of our headmistress. She was in her late fifties, a little woman dry as a winter twig, her face very tight, small and wary under a wig of coarse yellow hair. To pay for her board and lodging she taught deportment; in her youth she had been at the Court of the Tsar, and it was said that at sixteen years of age she was betrothed to a Russian nobleman. There was some sort of mystery here, about which all the girls were curious. Louise de Chausson said her mother had told her the story – how the nobleman, on the eve of his wedding, had shot himself through the head, having received word that certain speculations in which he had for many years been involved had come to light, and that his arrest was imminent ... 'And from that day,' Louise whispered, her prominent eyes gleaming in the candlelight, 'she began to wither and wither and wither away, till all her beauty was gone ...' Yes, I can see Louise now, kneeling upon her bed at the end of the vast dormitory, her thick plait hanging down over her nightgown, the little cross with the turquoise glittering at her beautiful and grainy throat. The others believed the story implicitly, except the piece about Mademoiselle Fournier's lost beauty. That they could not stomach. No, she was ugly as a monkey and had always been so.

For myself, I disbelieved in the nobleman; believed in the beauty. I have always had a curious faculty for stripping age from a face, recognizing the structure of the bone and the original texture of the skin beneath the disguisings of blotch, red vein and loosened flesh. When I looked at Mademoiselle Fournier I saw that the pinched and veinous nose had once been delicate and fine; that the sunken eyes had once been almond-shaped and blue; that the small, loose mouth had once pouted charmingly and opened upon romantic words. Why did I not believe in the nobleman? For no better reason than a distrust of Louise's information on any conceivable point. She was a terrible teller of falsehoods.

I was seventeen years old when I spent my last vacation at Bellançay, and knowing that my parents were to return to Europe in the following spring I watched the departure of the other girls with a heart not quite so heavy as was usual upon these occasions. In six months' time I, too, would be welcomed and loved, have adventures to relate and hopes upon which to feed.

I waved to them from a dormer window as they rattled away in *fiacre* and barouche down the drive between the beech trees, sired and damed, uncled and aunted, their boxes stacked high and their voices high as the treetops. They had never before seemed to me a particularly attractive group of girls – that is, not in the mass. There was, of course, Hélène de Courcey, with her great olive eyes; Madeleine Millet, whose pale red hair hung to her knees; but in the cluster they had no particular charm. That day, however, as, in new bonnets flowered and feathered and gauzed, they passed from sight down the narrowing file of beeches, I thought them all beautiful as princesses, and as princesses fortunate. Perhaps the nip in the air of a grey June made their cheeks rose-red, their eyes bright as the eyes of desirable young ladies in ballrooms.

The last carriage disappeared, the last sound died away. I turned from the window and went down the echoing stairs, flight after flight to the *salle à manger*, where my luncheon awaited me.

I ate alone. Mademoiselle Fournier took her meals in her own room upon the second floor, reading as she ate, crumbs falling from her lip on to the page. Tonight she and I, in the pattern of all holiday nights, would sit together for a while in the drawing-room before retiring.

'You don't make much of a meal, I must say,' Marie, the maid, rebuked me, as she cleared the plates. 'You can't afford to grow thinner, Mademoiselle, or you'll snap in two.' She brought me some cherries, which I would not eat then but preferred to take out with me in the garden. 'I'll wrap them up for you. No! you can't put them in your handkerchief like that; you'll stain it.'

She chattered to me for a while, in her good nature trying to ease my loneliness. Marie, at least, had relations in the village with whom she sometimes spent her evenings. 'What are you going to do with yourself, eh? Read your eyes out as usual?'

'I shall walk this afternoon, unless I find it too chilly.'

'You'll find it raining,' said Marie, cocking a calculating eye towards the high windows, 'in an hour. No, less; in half an hour.'

She busied herself wrapping up my cherries, which she handed to me in a neat parcel with a firm finger-loop of string. 'If it's wet you can play the piano.'

'You've forgotten,' I said, 'we have none now, or shan't have till they send the new one.'

Madame de Vallon had recently sold the old instrument, ugly and tinny, and with the money from the sale plus some money raised by parents' subscription had bought a grand pianoforte from Monsieur Oury, the mayor, whose eldest daughter, the musical one, had lately died.

'You can play on Mademoiselle Fournier's,' said Marie, 'she won't mind. You go and ask her.'

'What, is there another piano in the school?' I was amazed. I had been at Bellançay for seven years and had fancied no corner of the building unknown to me.

'Ah-ha,' said Marie triumphantly, 'there are still things you don't know, eh? You don't have to do the housework, or you'd be wiser.'

'But where is it?'

'In the empty schoolroom.'

I laughed at her. 'But they're all empty now! Whatever do you mean?'

'The one at the top,' she said impatiently, 'the one up the little flight of four stairs.'

'But that's the lumber room!'

'There's lumber in it. But it was a schoolroom once. It was when my aunt worked here. The piano's up there still, though *she* never plays it now.' Marie jerked her head skywards to indicate Mademoiselle Fournier upstairs.

I was fascinated by this information. We girls had never entered the lumber room because no attraction had been attached to it: to us it was simply a small, grimy door in the attic, locked we imagined, as we had never seen anyone go in or out. All we knew was that old books, valises, crates of unwanted china, were sometimes stacked up there out of the way.

There! I have failed to make my point quite clear. I must try again. *There was no mystery whatsoever attaching to this room,* which is the reason why no girl had ever tried the handle. Schoolgirls are curious and roaming creatures; how better can they be kept from a certain path than by the positive assurance that it is a *cul-de-sac*?

Dismissing Marie, I determined to go and seek permission from Mademoiselle Fournier to play upon her pianoforte. Since the departure of the old one, I had missed my music lessons and above all my practising; most of the girls were delighted to be saved a labour which to me, though I was an indifferent performer, had never been anything but a pleasure.

Mademoiselle had finished her meal and was just coming out upon the landing as I ran up the stairs to find her. I made my request.

She looked at me. 'Who told you about the instrument?'

'Marie.'

She was silent. Her brows moved up and down, moving the wig as they did so. It was a familiar trick with her when she was puzzled or annoyed. At last she said, without expression, 'No, you may not go up there,' and pushing me, hurried on downstairs.

At the turn of the staircase, however, she stopped and looked up. Her whole face was working with some unrecognizable emotion and her cheeks were burning red. 'Is there *no* place one can keep to oneself?' she cried at me furiously, and ducking her head, ran on.

When we sat that evening in the drawing-room, in our chairs turned to the fireless grate, she made no reference to the little scene of that afternoon. I thought she was, perhaps, sorry for having spoken so sharply: for she asked me a few personal questions of a kindly nature and just before bed-time brought out a tin box full of sugared almonds, which she shared with me.

She rose a little before I did, leaving me to retire when I chose. I stayed for perhaps half an hour in that vast, pale room with its moth-coloured draperies and its two tarnished chandeliers hanging a great way below the ceiling. Then I took up my candle and went to bed.

Now I must insist that I was a docile girl, a little sullen, perhaps, out of an unrealized resentment against my parents for (as I thought) deserting me; but obedient. I never had a bad conduct report from any of our teachers. It is important that this fact should be realized, so the reader shall know that what I did was not of my own free will.

I could not sleep. I lay open-eyed until my candle burned half-way down and the moon shifted round into the window-pane, weaving the golden light with its own blue-silver. I had no thought of any importance. Small pictures from the day's humdrum events flashed across my brain. I saw the neatly-looped parcel of cherries, the currant stain at the hem of Marie's apron, the starch-blue bird on the bonnet of Louise de Chausson, who had left Bellançay to marry an elderly and not very rich nobleman of Provence. I saw the leaves scurrying over the grey lawns, saw a woodpecker rapping at the trunk of the tree behind the house. What I did not see was the face of Mademoiselle Fournier up-turned from the stairway. She never entered my thoughts at all.

And so it is very strange that just before dawn I rose up, put on my dressing-gown and sought about the room until I found a pair of gloves my father had had made for me in India, fawn-coloured, curiously stitched in gold and dark green thread. These I took up, left the room and made my way silently up through the quiet house till I came to the door of the lumber room – or, as Marie had called it, the empty schoolroom. I paused with my hand upon the latch and listened. There was no sound except the impalpable breathing of the night, compound perhaps of the breathings of all who sleep, or perhaps of the movement of the moon through the gathered clouds.

I raised the latch gently and stepped within the room, closing the door softly behind me.

The chamber ran half-way across the length of the house at the rear of it, and was lighted by a ceiling window through which the moonrays poured lavishly down. It was still a schoolroom, despite the lumber stacked at the far end, the upright piano standing just behind the door. Facing me was a dais, on which stood a table and a chair. Before the dais were row upon row of desks, with benches behind. Everything was very dusty. With my finger I wrote DUST upon the teacher's table, then scuffed the word out again.

I went to the pianoforte. Behind the lattice-work was a ruching of torn red silk; the candle stumps in the sconces were red also. On the rack stood a piece of music, a Chopin nocturne simplified for beginners.

Gingerly I raised the lid and a mottled spider ran across the keys, dropped on hasty thread to the floor and ran away. The underside of the lid was completely netted by his silk; broken strands waved in the disturbed air and over the discoloured keys. As a rule I am afraid of spiders. That night I was not afraid. I laid my gloves on the keyboard, then closed the piano lid upon them.

I was ready to go downstairs. I took one glance about the room and for a moment thought I saw a shadowy form sitting upon one of the back benches, a form that seemed to weep. Then the impression passed away, and there was only the moonlight painting the room with its majesty. I went out, latched the door and crept back to my bed where, in the first colouring of dawn, I fell asleep.

Next day it was fine. I walked to the river in the morning, and in the afternoon worked at my *petit-point* upon the terrace. At tea-time an invitation came for me. The mayor, Monsieur Oury, wrote to Mademoiselle Fournier saying he believed there was a young lady left behind at school for the holidays, and that if she would care to dine at his house upon the following evening it would be a great pleasure to him and to his two young daughters. 'We are not a gay house these

87

days,' he wrote, 'but if the young lady cares for books and flowers there are a great number of both in my library and conservatory.'

'Shall I go?' I asked her.

'But of course! It is really a great honour for you. Do you know who the mayor's mother was before her marriage? She was a Uzès. Yes. And when she married Monsieur Oury's father, a very handsome man, her family cut her off with nothing at all and never spoke to her again. But they were very happy. You must wear your best gown and your white hat. Take the gown to Marie and she will iron it for you.'

The day upon which I was to visit Monsieur Oury was sunless and chilly. Plainly the blue dress that Marie had so beautifully spotted and pressed would not do at all. I had, however, a gown of fawn-coloured merino, plain but stylish, with which my brown straw hat would look very well.

Mademoiselle Fournier left the house at four o'clock to take tea with the village priest. She looked me over before she went, pinched my dress, tweaked it, pulled out the folds, and told me to sit quite still until the mayor's carriage came for me at half past six. 'Sit like a mouse, mind, or you will spoil the effect. Remember, Monsieur Oury is not nobody.' She said suddenly, 'Where are your gloves?'

I had forgotten them.

'Forgetting the very things that make a lady look a lady! Go and fetch them at once. Marie!'

The maid came in.

'Marie, see Mademoiselle's gloves are nice, and brush her down once more just as you see the carriage enter the drive. I mustn't wait now. Well, Maud, I wish you a pleasant evening. Don't forget you must be a credit to us.'

When she had gone Marie asked for my gloves. 'You'd better wear your brown ones with that hat, Mademoiselle.'

'Oh!' I exclaimed, 'I can't! I lost one of them on the expedition last week.'

'Your black, then?'

'They won't do. They'd look dreadful with this gown and hat. I know! I have a beautiful Indian pair that will match my dress exactly! I'll go and look for them.'

I searched. The reader must believe that I hunted all over my room for them anxiously, one eye upon the clock, though it was not yet twenty minutes past four. Chagrined, really upset at the thought of having my toilette ruined, I sat down upon the edge of the bed and began to cry a little. Tears came very easily to me in those lost and desolate days.

From high up in the house I heard a few notes of the piano, the melody of a Chopin nocturne played fumblingly in the treble, and I thought at once, 'Of course! The gloves are up there, where I hid them.'

The body warns us of evil before the senses are half awakened. I knew no fear as I ran lightly up towards the empty schoolroom, yet as I reached the door I felt a wave of heat engulf me, and knew a sick, nauseous stirring within my body. The notes, audible only to my ear (not to Marie's, for even at that moment I could hear her calling out some inquiry or gossip to the housekeeper), ceased. I lifted the latch and looked in.

The room appeared to be deserted, yet I could see the presence within it and know its distress. I peeped behind the door.

At the piano sat a terribly ugly, thin young girl in a dunce's cap. She was half turned towards me, and I saw her pig-like profile, the protruding teeth, the spurt of sandy eyelash. She wore a holland dress in the fashion of twenty years ago, and lean yellow streamers of hair fell down over her back from beneath the paper cone. Her hands, still resting on the fouled keyboard, were meshed about with the spider's web; beneath them lay my Indian gloves.

I made a movement towards the girl. She swivelled sharply and looked me full in the face. Her eyes were all white, red-rimmed, but tearless.

To get my gloves I must risk touching her. We looked at each other, she and I, and her head shrank low between her hunching shoulders. Somehow I must speak to her friendlily, disarm her while I gained my objective.

'Was it you playing?' I asked.

No answer. I closed my eyes. Stretching out my hands as in a game of blind man's buff, I sought for the keyboard.

'I have never heard you before,' I said.

I touched something: I did not know whether it was a glove or her dead hand.

'Have you been learning long?' I said. I opened my eyes. She was gone. I took my gloves, dusted off the webs and ran, ran so fast down the well of the house that on the last flight I stumbled and fell breathless into Marie's arms.

'Oh, I have had a fright! I have had a fright!'

She led me into the drawing-room, made me lie down, brought me a glass of wine.

'What is it, Mademoiselle? Shall I fetch the housekeeper? What has happened?'

But the first sip of wine had made me wary. 'I thought I saw someone hiding in my bedroom, a man. Perhaps a thief.'

At this the house was roused. Marie, the housekeeper and the gardener, who had not yet finished his work, searched every room (the lumber room, too, I think) but found nothing. I was scolded, petted, dosed, and Marie insisted, when the housekeeper was out of the way, on a *soupçon* of rouge on my cheeks because, she said, I could not upset Monsieur le Maire by looking like a dead body – he, poor man, having so recently had death in his house!

I recovered myself sufficiently to climb into the carriage, when it came, to comport myself decently on the drive, and to greet the mayor and his two daughters with dignity. Dinner, however, was a nightmare. My mind was so full of the horror I had seen that I could not eat – indeed I could barely force my trembling hand to carry the fork to my lips.

The mayor's daughters were only children, eleven and thirteen years old. At eight o'clock he bade them say good night to me and prepare for bed. When they had left us I told him I thought I had stayed long enough: but with a very grave look he placed his hand upon my arm and pressed me gently back into my chair.

'My dear young lady,' he said, 'I know your history, I know you are lonely and unhappy in France without your parents. Also I know that you have suffered some violent shock. Will you tell me about it and let me help you?'

The relief of his words, of his wise and kindly gaze, was too much for me. For the first time in seven years I felt fathered and in haven. I broke down and cried tempestuously, and he did not touch me or speak to me till I was a little more calm. Then he rang for the servant and told her to bring some lime-flower tea. When I had drunk and eaten some of the sweet cake that he urged upon me I told him about the empty schoolroom and of the horror which sat there at the webbed piano.

When I had done he was silent for a little while. Then he took both my hands in his.

'Mademoiselle,' he said, 'I am not going to blame you for the sin of curiosity; I think there was some strange compulsion upon you to act as you did. Therefore I mean to shed a little light upon this sad schoolroom by telling you the story of Mademoiselle Fournier.'

I started.

'No,' he continued restrainingly, 'you must listen quietly; and what I tell you you must never repeat to a soul save your own mother until both Mademoiselle Fournier and Madame de Vallon, her cousin, have passed away.'

I have kept this promise. They have been dead some fourteen years.

Monsieur Oury settled back in his chair. A tiny but comforting fire was lit in the grate, and the light of it was like a ring of guardian angels about us.

'Mademoiselle Fournier,' he began, 'was a very beautiful and proud young woman. Although she had no dowry, she was yet considered something of a *partie*, and in her nineteenth year she became affianced to a young Russian nobleman who at that time was living with his family upon an estate near Arles. His mother was not too pleased with the match, but she was a good woman, and she treated Charlotte – that is, Mademoiselle Fournier – with kindness. Just before the marriage Charlotte's father, who had been created a marquis by Bonaparte and now, by tolerance, held a minor government post under Louis Philippe, was found to have embezzled many thousands of francs.'

'Her father!' I could not help but exclaim.

Monsieur Oury smiled wryly. 'Legend has the lover for villain, eh? No; it was Aristide Fournier, a weak man, unable to stomach any recession in his fortunes. Monsieur Fournier shot himself as the gendarmes were on their way to take him. Charlotte, her marriage prospects destroyed, came near to lunacy. When she recovered from her long illness her beauty had gone. The mother of her ex-fiancé, in pity, suggested that a friend of hers, a lady at the Court of the Tsar, should employ Charlotte as governess to her children, and in Russia Charlotte spent nine years. She returned to France to assist her cousin with the school at Bellançay that Madame de Vallon had recently established.'

'Why did she return?' I said, less because I wished to know the answer than because I wished to break out of the veil of the past he was drawing about us both, and to feel myself a reality once more, Maud Arlett, aged seventeen years and nine months, brown hair and grey eyes, five foot seven and a half inches tall.

I did not succeed. The veil tightened, grew more opaque. 'Nobody knows. There were rumours. It seems not improbable that she was dismissed by her employer ... why, I don't know. It is an obscure period in Charlotte's history.'

He paused, to pour more tea for me.

'It was thought at first that Charlotte would be of great assistance to Madame de Vallon, teach all subjects and act as Madame's secretary. It transpired, however, that Charlotte was nervous to the point of sickness, and that she would grow less and less capable of teaching young girls. Soon she had no duties in the school except to give lessons in music and deportment.

'The music room was in the attic, which was then used as a schoolroom also. The pianoforte was Charlotte's own, one of the few things saved from the wreck of her home.'

Monsieur Oury rose and walked out of the ring of firelight. He stood gazing out of the window, now beaded by a thin rain, and his voice grew out of the dusk as the music of waves grows out of the sea. 'I shall tell you the rest briefly, Mademoiselle. It distresses me to tell it to you at all, but I think I can help you in no other way.

'A young girl came to the school, a child; perhaps twelve or thirteen years of age. Her mother and father were in the

East, and she was left alone, even during the vacations – '

'Like myself!' I cried.

'Yes, like yourself; and I have an idea that that is why she chose you for her ... *confidante.*'

I shuddered.

He seemed to guess at my movement for, turning from the window, he returned to the firelight and to me.

'In one way, however, she was unlike you as can possibly be imagined, Mademoiselle.' He smiled with a faint, sad gallantry. 'She was exceedingly ugly.'

'From the first, Charlotte took a dislike to her, and it grew to mania. The child, Thérèse Dasquier, was never very intelligent; in Charlotte's grip she became almost imbecile. Charlotte was always devising new punishments, new humiliations. Thérèse became the mock and the pity of the school.'

'But Madame de Vallon, couldn't she have stopped it?' I interrupted indignantly.

'My dear,' Monsieur Oury replied sadly, 'like many women of intellect – she is, as you know, a fine teacher – she is blind to most human distress. She is, herself, a kind woman: she believes others are equally kind, cannot believe there could be ... suffering ... torment ... going on beneath her very nose. Has she ever realized *your* loneliness, Mademoiselle, given you any motherly word, or ...? I thought not. But I am digressing, and that I must not do. We have talked too much already.

'One night Thérèse Dasquier arose quietly, crept from the dormitory and walked barefooted a mile and a half in the rain across the fields to the river, where she drowned herself.'

'Oh, God,' I murmured, my heart cold and heavy as a stone.

'God, I think,' said Monsieur Oury, 'cannot have been attentive at that time ...' His face changed. He added hastily,

'And God forgive me for judging Him. We cannot know – we cannot guess ...' he continued rapidly, in a dry, rather high voice oddly unlike his own. 'There was scandal, great scandal. Thérèse's parents returned to France and everyone expected them to force the truth to light. They turned out to be frivolous and selfish people, who could scarcely make even a parade of grief for a child they had never desired and whose death they could not regret. Thérèse was buried and forgotten. Slowly, very slowly, the story also was forgotten. After all, nobody *knew* the truth, they could only make conjecture.'

'Then how did you know?' I cried out.

'Because Madame de Vallon came to me in bitter distress with the tale of the rumours and besought me to clear Charlotte's name. You see, she simply could not believe a word against her. And at the same time the aunt of Marie, the maid, came to me swearing she could prove the truth of the accusations ... Three days afterwards she was killed in the fire which destroyed the old quarter of Bellançay.'

I looked my inquiry into his face.

'I knew which of the women spoke the truth,' he replied, answering me, 'because in Madame de Vallon's face I saw concern for her own blood. In the other woman's I saw concern for a child who to her was nothing.'

'But still, you *guessed*!' I protested.

He turned upon me his long and grave regard. 'You,' he said, '*you* do not know the truth? Even you?'

I do not know how I endured the following weeks in that lonely school. I remember how long I lay shivering in my bed, staring into the flame of the candle because I felt that in the brightest part of it alone was refuge, how the sweat jumped out from my brow at the least sound in the stillness of midnight, and how, towards morning, I would fall into some morose and terrible dream of dark stairways and locked doors.

Yet, as day by day, night by night, went by with no untoward happening, my spirit knew some degree of easing and I began once more to find comfort in prayer – that is, I dared once again to cover my face while I repeated 'Our Father', and to rise from my knees without fear of what might be standing patiently at my shoulder.

The holidays drew to an end. 'Tomorrow,' said Mademoiselle Fournier, folding her needlework in preparation for bed, 'your companions will be back with you once more. You'll like that, eh?'

Ever since my request and her refusal, she had been perfectly normal in her manner – I mean, she had been normally sour, polite, withdrawn.

'I shall like it,' I sighed, 'only too well.'

She smiled remotely. 'I am not a lively companion for you, Maud, I fear. Still, I am as I am. I am too old to change myself.'

She went on upstairs, myself following, our candles smoking in the draught and our shadows prancing upon the wall.

I said my prayers and read for a little while. I was unusually calm, feeling safety so nearly within my reach that I need be in no hurry to stretch out my hand and grasp it tight. The bed seemed softer than usual, the sheets sweet-smelling, delicately warm and light. I fell into a dreamless sleep.

I awoke suddenly to find the moon full on my face. I sat up, dazzled by her light, a strange feeling of energy tingling in my body. 'What is it,' I whispered, 'that I must do?'

The moon shone broadly on the great surfaces of gleaming wood, on the bureau, the tallboy, the wardrobe, flashed upon the mirror, sparkled on the spiralling bedposts. I slipped out of bed and in my nightgown went out into the passage.

It was very bright and still. Below me, the stairs fell steeply to the tessellated entrance hall. To my right the passage narrowed to the door behind which Mademoiselle Fournier slept, her wig upon a candlestick, her book and her spectacles lying on the rug at her side – so Marie had described her to me. Before me the stairs rose to the turn of the landing, from which a further flight led to the second floor, the third floor and the attics. The wall above the stair rail was white with the moon.

I felt the terror creeping up beneath my calm, though only as one might feel the shadow of pain while in the grip of a drug. I was waiting now as I had been instructed to wait, and I knew for what. I stared upwards, my gaze fastened upon the turn of the stairs.

Then, upon the moonlit wall, there appeared the shadow of a cone.

She stood just out of sight, her fool's-capped head nodding forward, listening even as I was listening.

I held my breath. My forehead was ice-cold.

She came into view then, stepping carefully, one hand upholding a corner of her skirt, the other feeling its way along the wall. As she reached me I closed my eyes. I felt her pass by, knew she had gone along the passage to the room of Mademoiselle Fournier. I heard a door quietly opened and shut.

In those last moments of waiting my fear left me, though I could move neither hand nor foot. My ears were sharp for the least sound.

It came: a low and awful cry, tearing through the quiet of the house and blackening the moonlight itself. The door opened again.

She came hastening out, and in the shadow of the cap she smiled. She ran on tiptoe past me, up the stairs.

The last sound? I thought it had been the death cry of Mademoiselle Fournier; but there was yet another.

As Marie and the housekeeper came racing down, white-faced, from their rooms (they must have passed her as she stood in the shade) I heard very distinctly the piping voice of a young girl:

'*Tiens, Mademoiselle, je vous remercie beaucoup!*'

We went together, Marie, the housekeeper and I, into the room of Charlotte Fournier, and only I did not cry out when we looked upon the face.

'You see,' said Monsieur Oury, on the day I left Bellançay for ever to join my parents in Paris, 'she did make you her *confidante*. She gave to you the privilege of telling her story and publishing her revenge. Are you afraid of her now, knowing that there was no harm in her for *you*, knowing that she has gone for ever, to trouble no house again?'

'I am not afraid,' I said, and I believed it was true; but even now I cannot endure to awaken suddenly on moonlit nights, and I fling my arms about my husband and beg him to rouse up and speak with me until the dawn.

The Invisible Boy

RAY BRADBURY

She took the great iron spoon and the mummified frog and gave it a bash and made dust of it, and talked to the dust while she ground it in her stony fists quickly. Her beady gray bird-eyes flickered at the cabin. Each time she looked, a head in the small thin window ducked as if she'd fired off a shotgun.

'Charlie!' cried Old Lady. 'You must come outa there! I'm fixing a lizard magic to unlock that rusty door! You come out now and I won't make the earth shake or the trees go up in fire or the sun set at high noon!'

The only sound was the warm mountain light on the high turpentine trees, a tufted squirrel chittering around and around on a green-furred log, the ants moving in a fine brown line at Old Lady's bare, blue-veined feet.

'You been starving in there two days, darn you!' she panted, chiming the spoon against a flat rock, causing the plump gray miracle bag to swing at her waist. Sweating sour, she rose and marched at the cabin, bearing the pulverized flesh. 'Come out now!' She flicked a pinch of powder inside the lock. 'All right, I'll come get you!' she wheezed.

She spun the knob with one walnut-coloured hand, first one way, then the other. 'O Lord,' she intoned, 'fling this door wide!'

When nothing flung, she added yet another philtre and

99

held her breath. Her long blue untidy skirt rustled as she peered into her bag of darkness to see if she had any scaly monsters there, any charm finer than the frog she'd killed months ago for such a crisis as this.

She heard Charlie breathing against the door. His folks had pranced off into some Ozark town early this week, leaving him, and he'd run almost six miles to Old Lady for company – she was by way of being an aunt or cousin or some such, and he didn't mind her fashions.

But then, two days ago, Old Lady, having gotten used to the boy around, decided to keep him for convenient company. She pricked her thin shoulder bone, drew out three blood pearls, spat wet over her right elbow, tromped on a crunch-cricket, and at the same instant clawed her left hand at Charlie, crying, 'My son you are, you are my son, for all eternity!'

Charlie, bounding like a startled hare, had crashed off into the bush, heading for home.

But Old Lady, skittering quick as a gingham lizard, cornered him in a dead end, and Charlie holed up in his old hermit's cabin and wouldn't come out, no matter how she whammed door, window, or knothole with amber-coloured fist or trounced her ritual fires, explaining to him that he was certainly her son *now*, all right.

'Charlie, you *there*?' she asked, cutting holes in the door planks with her bright little slippery eyes.

'I'm all of me here,' he replied finally, very tired.

Maybe he would fall out on the ground any moment. She wrestled the knob hopefully. Perhaps a pinch too much frog powder had grated the lock wrong. She always overdid or underdid her miracles, she mused angrily, never doing them just *exact*, Devil take it!

'Charlie, I only wants someone to night-prattle to,

someone to warm hands with at the fire. Someone to fetch kindling for me mornings, and fight off the spunks that come creeping of early fogs! I ain't got no fetching on you for myself, son, just for your company.' She smacked her lips. 'Tell you what, Charles, you come out and I *teach* you things!'

'What things?' he suspicioned.

'Teach you how to buy cheap, sell high. Catch a snow weasel, cut off its head, carry it warm in your hind pocket. There!'

'Aw,' said Charlie.

She made haste. 'Teach you to make yourself shotproof. So if anyone bangs at you with a gun, nothing happens.'

When Charlie stayed silent, she gave him the secret in a high fluttering whisper. 'Dig and stitch mouse-ear roots on Friday during full moon, and wear 'em around your neck in a white silk.'

'You're crazy,' Charlie said.

'Teach you how to stop blood or make animals stand frozen or make blind horses see, all them things I'll teach you! Teach you to cure a swelled-up cow and unbewitch a goat. Show you how to make yourself invisible!'

'Oh,' said Charlie.

Old Lady's heart beat like a Salvation tambourine.

The knob turned from the other side.

'You,' said Charlie, 'are funning me.'

'No, I'm not,' exclaimed Old Lady. 'Oh, Charlie, why, I'll make you like a window, see right through you. Why, child, you'll be surprised!'

'Real invisible?'

'Real invisible!'

'You won't fetch on to me if I walk out?'

'Won't touch a bristle of you, son.'

'Well,' he drawled reluctantly, 'all right.'

101

The door opened. Charlie stood in his bare feet, head down, chin against chest. 'Make me invisible,' he said.

'First we got to catch us a bat,' said Old Lady. 'Start lookin'!'

She gave him some jerky beef for his hunger and watched him climb a tree. He went high up and high up and it was nice seeing him there and it was nice having him here and all about after so many years alone with nothing to say good morning to but bird-droppings and silvery snail tracks.

Pretty soon a bat with a broken wing fluttered down out of the tree. Old Lady snatched it up, beating warm and shrieking between its porcelain white teeth, and Charlie dropped down after it, hand upon clenched hand, yelling.

That night, with the moon nibbling at the spiced pine cones, Old Lady extracted a long silver needle from under her wide blue dress. Gumming her excitement and secret anticipation, she sighted up the dead bat and held the cold needle steady-steady.

She had long ago realized that her miracles, despite all perspirations and salts and sulphurs, failed. But she had always dreamt that one day the miracles might start functioning, might spring up in crimson flowers and silver stars to prove that God had forgiven her for her pink body and her pink thoughts and her warm body and her warm thoughts as a young miss. But so far God had made no sign and said no word, but nobody knew this except Old Lady.

'Ready?' she asked Charlie, who crouched cross-kneed, wrapping his pretty legs in long goose-pimpled arms, his mouth open, making teeth. 'Ready,' he whispered, shivering.

'There!' She plunged the needle deep in the bat's right eye. 'So!'

'Oh!' screamed Charlie, wadding up his face.

'Now I wrap it in gingham, and here, put it in your pocket, keep it there, bat and all. Go on!'

He pocketed the charm.

'Charlie!' she shrieked fearfully. 'Charlie, where *are* you? I can't *see* you, child!'

'Here!' He jumped so the light ran in red streaks up his body. 'I'm here, Old Lady!' He stared wildly at his arms, legs, chest, and toes. 'I'm here!'

Her eyes looked as if they were watching a thousand fireflies criss-crossing each other in the wild night air.

'Charlie, oh, you went *fast*! Quick as a hummingbird! Oh, Charlie, come *back* to me!'

'But I'm *here*!' he wailed.

'Where?'

'By the fire, the fire! And – and I can see myself. I'm not invisible at all!'

Old lady rocked on her lean flanks. 'Course *you* can see *you*! Every invisible person knows himself. Otherwise, how could you eat, walk, or get around places? Charlie, touch me. Touch me so I *know* you.'

Uneasily he put out a hand.

She pretended to jerk, startled, at his touch. '*Ah!*'

'You mean to say you can't *find* me?' he asked. 'Truly?'

'Not the least half rump of you!'

She found a tree to stare at, and stared at it with shining eyes, careful not to glance at him. 'Why, I sure *did* a trick *that* time!' She sighed with wonder. 'Whooeee. Quickest invisible I *ever* made! Charlie. Charlie, how you *feel*?'

'Like creek water – all stirred.'

'You'll settle.'

Then after a pause she added, 'Well, what you going to do now, Charlie, since you're invisible?'

All sorts of things shot through his brain, she could tell. Adventures stood up and danced like hell-fire in his eyes, and his mouth, just hanging, told what it meant to be a boy who imagined himself like the mountain winds. In a cold dream he said, 'I'll run across wheat fields, climb snow mountains, steal white chickens off'n farms. I'll kick pink pigs when they ain't looking. I'll pinch pretty girls' legs when they sleep, snap their garters in schoolrooms.' Charlie looked at Old Lady, and from the shiny tips of her eyes she saw something wicked shape his face. 'And other things I'll do, I'll do, I will,' he said.

'Don't try nothing on me,' warned Old Lady. 'I'm brittle as spring ice and I don't take handling.' Then: 'What about your folks?'

'My folks?'

'You can't fetch yourself home looking like that. Scare the inside ribbons out of them. Your mother'd faint straight back like timber falling. Think they want you about the house to stumble over and your ma having to call you every three minutes, even though you're in the room next her elbow?'

Charlie had not considered it. He sort of simmered down and whispered out a little 'Gosh' and felt of his long bones carefully.

'You'll be mighty lonesome. People looking through you like a water glass, people knocking you aside because they didn't reckon you to be underfoot. And women, Charlie, *women* –'

He swallowed. 'What about women?'

'No woman will be giving you a second stare. And no woman wants to be kissed by a boy's mouth they can't even *find*!'

Charlie dug his bare toe in the soil contemplatively. He pouted. 'Well, I'll stay invisible, anyway, for a spell. I'll have me some fun. I'll just be pretty careful, is all. I'll stay out from in front of wagons and horses and Pa. Pa shoots at the nariest sound.' Charlie blinked. 'Why, with me invisible, someday Pa might just up and fill me with buckshot, thinkin' I was a hill squirrel in the doorway. Oh . . .'

Old Lady nodded at a tree. 'That's likely.'

'Well,' he decided slowly, 'I'll stay invisible for tonight, and tomorrow you can fix me back all whole again, Old Lady.'

'Now if that ain't just like a critter, always wanting to be what he can't be,' remarked Old Lady to a beetle on a log.

'What you mean?' said Charlie.

'Why,' she explained, 'it was real hard work, fixing you up. It'll take a little *time* for it to wear off. Like a coat of paint wears off, boy.'

'You!' he cried. 'You did this to me! Now you make me back, you make me seeable!'

'Hush,' she said. 'It'll wear off, a hand or a foot at a time.'

'How'll it look, me around the hills with just one hand showing!'

'Like a five-winged bird hopping on the stones and bramble.'

'Or a foot showing!'

'Like a small pink rabbit jumping thicket.'

'Or my head floating!'

'Like a hairy balloon at the carnival!'

'How long before I'm *whole*?' he asked.

She deliberated that it might pretty well be an entire year.

He groaned. He began to sob and bite his lips and make fists. 'You magicked me, you did this, you did this thing to me. Now I won't be able to run home!'

She winked. 'But you *can* stay here, child, stay on with me real comfort-like, and I'll keep you fat and saucy.'

He flung it out: 'You did this on purpose! You mean old hag, you want to keep me here!'

He ran off through the shrubs on the instant.

'Charlie, come back!'

No answer but the pattern of his feet on the soft dark turf, and his wet choking cry which passed swiftly off and away.

She waited and then kindled herself a fire. 'He'll be back,' she whispered. And thinking inward on herself, she said, 'And now I'll have me my company through spring and into late summer. Then, when I'm tired and want a silence, I'll send him home.'

Charlie returned noiselessly with the first gray of dawn, gliding over the rimed turf to where Old Lady sprawled like a bleached stick before the scattered ashes.

He sat on some creek pebbles and stared at her.

She didn't dare look at him or beyond. He had made no sound, so how could she know he was anywhere about? She couldn't.

He sat there, tear marks on his cheeks.

Pretending to be just waking – but she had found no sleep from one end of the night to the other – Old Lady stood up, grunting and yawning, and turned in a circle to the dawn.

'Charlie?'

Her eyes passed from pines to soil, to sky, to the far hills. She called out his name, over and over again, and she felt like staring plumb straight at him, but she stopped herself. 'Charlie? Oh, Charles!' she called, and heard the echoes say the very same.

He sat, beginning to grin a bit, suddenly, knowing he was close to her, yet she must feel alone. Perhaps he felt the growing of a secret power, perhaps he felt secure from the world, certainly he was *pleased* with his invisibility.

She said aloud, 'Now where *can* that boy be? If he only made a noise so I could tell just where he is, maybe I'd fry him a breakfast.'

She prepared the morning victuals, irritated at his continuous quiet. She sizzled bacon on a hickory stick. 'The smell of it will draw his nose,' she muttered.

While her back was turned he swiped all the frying bacon and devoured it tastily.

She whirled, crying out, 'Lord!'

She eyed the clearing suspiciously. 'Charlie, that *you*?'

Charlie wiped his mouth clean on his wrists.

She trotted about the clearing, making like she was trying to locate him. Finally, with a clever thought, acting blind, she headed straight for him, groping. 'Charlie, where *are* you?'

A lightning streak, he evaded her, bobbing, ducking.

It took her all her will power not to give chase; but you can't chase invisible boys, so she sat down, scowling, sputtering, and tried to fry more bacon. But every fresh strip she cut he would steal bubbling off the fire and run away far. Finally, cheeks burning, she cried, 'I know where you are! Right *there*! I hear you run!' She pointed to one side of him, not too accurate. He ran again. 'Now you're there!' she shouted. 'There, and there!' pointing to all the places he was in the next five minutes. 'I hear you press a grass blade, knock a flower, snap a twig. I got fine shell ears, delicate as roses. They can hear the stars moving!'

Silently he galloped off among the pines, his voice trailing back, 'Can't hear me when I'm set on a rock. I'll just *set*!'

All day he sat on an observatory rock in the clear wind, motionless and sucking his tongue.

Old Lady gathered wood in the deep forest, feeling his eyes weaseling on her spine. She wanted to babble: 'Oh, I see you, I see you! I was only fooling about invisible boys! You're right there!' But she swallowed her gall and gummed it tight.

The following morning he did the spiteful things. He began leaping from behind trees. He made toad-faces, frog-faces, spider-faces at her, clenching down his lips with his fingers, popping his raw eyes, pushing up his nostrils so you could peer in and see his brain thinking.

Once she dropped her kindling. She pretended it was a blue jay startled her.

He made a motion as if to strangle her.

She trembled a little.

He made another move as if to bang her shins and spit on her cheek.

These motions she bore without a lid-flicker or a mouth-twitch.

He stuck out his tongue, making strange bad noises. He wiggled his loose ears so she wanted to laugh, and finally she did laugh and explained it away quickly by saying, 'Sat on a salamander! Whew, how it poked!'

By high noon the whole madness boiled to a terrible peak.

For it was at that exact hour that Charlie came racing down the valley stark boy-naked!

Old Lady nearly fell flat with shock!

'Charlie!' she almost cried.

Charlie raced naked up one side of a hill and naked down the other – naked as day, naked as the moon, raw as the sun and a newborn chick, his feet shimmering and rushing like the wings of a low-skimming hummingbird.

Old Lady's tongue locked in her mouth. What could she say? Charlie, go dress? For *shame*? *Stop* that? *Could* she?

Oh, Charlie, Charlie, God! Could she say that now? *Well?*

Upon the big rock, she witnessed him dancing up and down, naked as the day of his birth, stomping bare feet, smacking his hands on his knees and sucking in and out his white stomach like blowing and deflating a circus balloon.

She shut her eyes tight and prayed.

After three hours of this she pleaded, 'Charlie, Charlie, come here! I got something to *tell* you!'

Like a fallen leaf he came, dressed again, praise the Lord.

'Charlie,' she said, looking at the pine trees, 'I see your right toe. *There* it is.'

'You do?' he said.

'Yes,' she said very sadly. 'There it is like a horny toad on the grass. And there, up there's your left ear hanging on the air like a pink butterfly.'

Charlie danced. 'I'm forming in, I'm forming in!'

Old Lady nodded. 'Here comes your ankle!'

'Gimme *both* my feet!' ordered Charlie.

'You got 'em.'

'How about my hands?'

'I see one crawling on your knee like a daddy longlegs.'

'How about the other one?'

'It's crawling too.'

'I got a body?'

'Shaping up fine.'

'I'll need my head to go home, Old Lady.'

To go home, she thought wearily. 'No!' she said, stubborn and angry. 'No, you ain't got no head. No head at all,' she cried. She'd leave that to the very last. 'No head, no head,' she insisted.

'No head?' he wailed.

'Yes, oh my God, yes, yes, you got your blamed head!' she

109

snapped, giving up. 'Now, fetch me back my bat with the needle in his eye!'

He flung it at her. 'Haaaa-yoooo!' His yelling went all up the valley, and long after he had run towards home she heard his echoes, racing.

Then she plucked up her kindling with a great dry weariness and started back toward her shack, sighing, talking. And Charlie followed her all the way, *really* invisible now, so she couldn't see him, just hear him, like a pine cone dropping or a deep underground stream trickling, or a squirrel clambering a bough; and over the fire at twilight she and Charlie sat, him so invisible, and her feeding him bacon he wouldn't take, so she ate it herself, and then she fixed some magic and fell asleep with Charlie, made out of sticks and rags and pebbles, but still warm and her very own son, slumbering and nice in her shaking mother arms ... and they talked about golden things in drowsy voices until dawn made the fire slowly, slowly wither out ...

Acknowledgements

The editor and publishers gratefully acknowledge the following for permission to reproduce copyright stories in this book:

'The Day We Threw the Switch on Georgie Tozer' copyright © Brian Alderson 1980, reprinted from an article first published in *The Times*; 'Sonia Plays a Record' copyright © Jon Blake 1990, first published in this collection; 'The Invisible Boy' reprinted by permission of Don Congdon Associates, Inc., copyright © 1945, renewed by Ray Bradbury 1972; 'The Fly' copyright © Joyce Dunbar 1990, first published in this collection; 'Fabric Crafts' copyright © Anne Fine 1990, first published in this collection; 'Pictures' copyright © Toby Forward 1987, first published by Virago Press Limited 1987 under the title 'Down the Road, Worlds Away' by 'Rahila Khan', reproduced by permission of Simon & Schuster Young Books, UK; 'The Empty Schoolroom' copyright © Pamela Hansford Johnson, first recorded publication 1969, reprinted by permission of Curtis Brown Ltd on behalf of the Estate of Pamela Hansford Johnson; 'The Rescue of Karen Arscott' copyright © Gene Kemp 1982, first published in the collection *School's OK* published by Evans Brothers Limited; 'Teeth' copyright © Jan Mark 1984, first published by Puffin Books in *Hundreds and Hundreds* edited by Peter Dickinson; 'Gypsy' copyright © Sam McBratney, first printed by Puffin Books in *The Genius and Other Irish Stories* 1988; 'A Christmas Pudding Improves with Keeping' copyright © Philippa Pearce 1978, first published by Viking Kestrel in *Whose Afraid? and Other Strange Stories*.